AF708809

THE SELLING OF GENERAL ELECTRIC

to Tom
Good friend and
former colleague.

4/29/90

THE SELLING OF GENERAL ELECTRIC

An insider's view from GE's Advertising and Sales Promotion Department, for more than a century the largest in-house advertising agency in the world.

by

James R. Burnside

High Peaks Press

Copyright © 1990 by James R. Burnside.

All rights reserved.
No part of this publication may be
reproduced or transmitted in any form
or by any means, electronic or mechanical,
including photocopy, recording, or any
information storage or retrieval
system, without permission in writing
from the publisher.

International Standard Book Number: 0-9624923-0-2

Library of Congress Catalog Card Number: 89-51860

High Peaks Press
2307 Cayuga Road
Schenectady, New York 12309

Printed in the United States of America.

to Carl Ally

who, as an A&SP trainee, used to brown-bag it at noon while flying an Air National Guard P-47 Thunderbolt from the Schenectady County Airport. In an understatement, rare for the future member of the Advertising Hall of Fame, Carl noted: "Beats the GE cafeteria."

CONTENTS

FOREWORD

Every couple of years, usually on the odd year, several hundred expatriates from the General Electric Company gather in New York City, as they have over more than two decades, for a luncheon meeting of the GE Alumni Club.

The assembly reaffirms a sort of mystical loyalty that pulls together people who left the fold to serve corporate America, as they did at GE, in posts ranging from the boardroom to the bullpen.

Regardless of what they did at GE, all shared a common mission – to market, promote and sell the products, services and people of GE. And, always, the company itself, which has been lauded as a marketing pioneer and one of the best managed companies in America.

The common thread of that GE selling process was communications. And from the very beginnings of the company until late in the '80s, most of it was generated down in the engine room of GE communications called the Advertising and Sales Promotion Department.

As GE's in-house agency, A&SP* at its peak would have ranked among the top 20 advertising agencies in the world, if its billings were capitalized like those of its peers on the outside.

Nearly half of those who attend the Alumni Club meetings began their careers in A&SP. Those who did not at least rubbed shoulders with A&SPers. It was virtually impossible for anyone to initiate communications from within GE for any length of time without being involved in some way with A&SP.

A&SP has always fascinated the business and marketing world. Serving all segments of GE, it was a microcosm of the company itself. GE, in turn, mirrors pretty well the ups and downs of the U.S. economy, as measured by the Gross National Product, or GNP. The company manufactures products in two thirds of the Standard Industry Classifications (SICs) and sells to all of them.

---

*While many alumni remember it as the A&SP Department, it has undergone various name changes. In its last form GE called it Corporate Market Programs.

This unique marketing and promotional arena is the clue as to why A&SP veterans are so much in demand throughout industry and business. The roster of a recent Alumni Club meeting reflects the glittering talents of those who left GE after being in A&SP, let alone those who served elsewhere in the far reaches of the company.

The listing shows that 33 A&SP alumni are presidents or CEOs of advertising agencies, while another 36 hold the same posts in other areas of commerce and industry. In addition, 102 have the title of vice president, and a couple of dozen more are directors or managers of advertising.

Ex-A&SPers hold management positions in half of the top 20 advertising agencies in the country. They are in half of the top 12 Fortune 500 companies, and in 20% of the top 100.

Canvass ad agencies around the country, and you'll find a sprinkling of A&SPers throughout. The roster of the New York City club shows they're in 17 agencies in that city, in half again as many in Connecticut, and in 32 agencies in 15 other states as well as Switzerland, Singapore and Hong Kong.

A good many ex-A&SPers started their own agencies. Probably the best known in Manhattan is Carl Ally, named to the Advertising Hall of Fame in 1962; he started the agency which became Ally & Gargano/MCA. Coming from Campbell-Ewald, he slashed a path through the pedestrian ad world with pioneering comparative campaigns for Federal Express ("When it absolutely, positively has to be there overnight"), MCI, Commodore, Volvo and Hertz ("For years, Avis has been telling you Hertz is No. 1. Now, we're going to tell you why"). Carl is now an international advertising consultant.

Another ex-A&SPer, Henry Schachte, rose to become CEO of J. Walter Thompson. Today, many other major agencies have enlisted ex-A&SP staff executives, such as Peter Falcone, President of DDB Needham Worldwide, and Tom Yobbagy, Executive VP and Creative Director of Doyle Dane Bernbach, Inc. At an early Alumni Club meeting someone noted that six of the eight senior vice presidents then at Marsteller were A&SP graduates.

Think of recent IBM campaigns you've seen in consumer and trade media; they were likely the work of ex-A&SPers. Bob Wells, now Senior Vice President and Managing Director at Lord, Einstein, O'Neill & Partners in New York City, supervised the Charlie Chaplin campaign for IBM while in the same post for Lord, Geller, Federico, Einstein. Bill Muir directs the preparation of IBM sales promotion as head and founder of Muir Cornelius Moore, now a unit of Interpublic's Lintas:Worldwide.

In 1983, *Adweek* magazine rated Muir's agency and Lord Geller the top two "hottest eastern agencies," with Ally in fourth place.

Enter the photographic world, and two ex-A&SPers contributed competing views there. Bill Mick, while at J. Walter Thompson, helped guide Kodak into the copier and duplicator market, while Lynn Keiser touted the wares of Polaroid as a member of that firm's advertising staff.

Look around the business world, and you'll find A&SPers in lofty reaches. There's Lee Guittar, who went from publisher of the *Dallas Times-Herald* to the presidency of *USA Today,* then to his present post as Vice President and Group Executive of the Hearst Corporation. There's J. Byron Felter, who's Group VP-Sales of U.S. Grocery Products for Quaker Oats.

Then there's Morgan Hunter, who winnowed his way through Procter & Gamble and American Cyanamid to become president of R. J. Reynolds and then Scott Paper; he retired in mid-1989 as Managing Partner of MarketCorp Ventures. One who missed by a whisker was merely a client of A&SP – Bob Fredericks, the last CEO of RCA, who came out of GE consumer advertising in Louisville.

And, of course, there's the most memorable skywalker of them all, J. Stanford Smith, former general manager of A&SP, who was invited to speak to the Alumni Club in 1968 before he even left GE. He rose through a variety of line and staff jobs to GE senior vice president, then left to become CEO of International Paper.

The next time you vacation in Vermont for skiing or shopping, stop in Manchester to visit one of the most successful gift shops in New England, the Jelly Mill; you'll be greeted by owner and ex-A&SPer Clint Lewis. While you're at it, climb to the fourth floor and say hello to ex-A&SPer Bill Herrick, in his studio, The Incredible Tree. Bill left A&SP in 1955 with Frank Muller and John Jordan to start the forerunner of Muller Jordan Weiss in New York City, then quit in the early '70s to sculpt wood in the peace of the country.

And, there's a fugitive from the Schenectady GE news bureau named Kurt Vonnegut, Jr. who's had some success at writing, though not in advertising. The acclaimed novelist was honored as Man of the Year at the Club's 1983 meeting, as was Lee Guittar in 1985.

The spirit of the GE Alumni Club isn't an aberration limited to New York City. Enthusiasm keeps filtering back from such venturesome alumni as agency principals Chuck Roberts of Roberts/Mealer/Emerson in Costa Mesa, CA; Tom Hougan of Gerber Advertising, Portland, OR; and Bob Allison of Doe Anderson in Louisville.

The word from Jim Grafton, manager of public relations for Boeing's Aerospace Company in Seattle prior to his recent retirement, is typical. Following a return visit to Schenectady a couple of years back, he said: "We have enough people out here for a club, but just haven't gotten our act together. I'm dying to attend a meeting somewhere."

Or, this one from H. Zane Robbins, an agency principal in Chicago: "Don't send me any more of these retirement notices. Every time I think back on the old days and the old friends, I'm tempted to send in a résumé. I'd be flattered to think I'm missed just half as much as I miss you guys."

There aren't any records on how many GE alumni are still out there, but the number has got to be considerable.

For more than 30 years after World War II, A&SP flooded the GE arena with a staff of 400 to 500 specialists, peaking one year at more than 800. New blood kept pouring in from A&SP recruitment at colleges and universities across the U.S. In a typical year, A&SP would contact 2500, interview 1500, and hire 50.

I was one of 39 hired by A&SP in 1948, and was the last of that class to leave, as Creative Director in Albany, NY, in 1985. Over the years, a lot of the alumni kept in touch, and the questions to me were always the same: What's going on at GE? Who's left? And, what's it like now?

There seem to be a couple of factors behind all this interest. The first is the nature of the creature itself.

A&SP inherited the genes of its parent – it was always a highly charged organism, usually growing, sometimes retracting, but always in the thick of whatever was going on . . . often way out front of the rest of GE. A&SP was highly successful in almost everything it tried. It surmounted every major sales challenge but the last, when it tried to convince Jack Welch it was indispensable to his call for a Marketing Renaissance.

A&SP was also imperfect, like the company and, up close, its flaws were magnified. When a person left, he or she then had something to compare it with. It became immediately clear that A&SP rated pretty well. It did everything the typical agency does, but a lot more. A&SP was something out of the ordinary, a thing of wonder which became layered with nostalgia as the years went by, like an old flame from high school.

The second thing that draws people back is the mystique of GE. One of the classic quotes from the 1972 Club meeting was: "There are three great experiences available on earth – the Roman Catholic Church, the Mafia, and General Electric."

Even sociologists recognize there's something to it. One told GE's former chairman, Reg Jones: "Your company has developed its own subculture. You acculturate your people – unconsciously indoctrinate them into your special value system, show them how to work together and live together in your own distinctive community – even though it's spread all around the world."

Jones agrees: "When people leave General Electric, they never stop talking about it. They form alumni groups. They try to change their companies to fit the General Electric style. And if they come back they always say, 'God, it's good to be back among the professionals!' If I've heard that once, I've heard it a thousand times."

Not everyone will agree with this. But for those who do, and for those who maybe just want to know what the ruckus is about, this will fill you in on what went on at GE, and at A&SP, up until the end.

This isn't a history; there are various zigs and zags that intrude on the chronological flow. Rather, the intent is to look at things in the context of what moved the General Electric Company.

That's why, after all, the happenings at A&SP have always been so informative, entertaining, and possibly instructive.

Schenectady, New York
January 1990

ACKNOWLEDGMENTS

I used to read *The New Yorker* but gave it up on facing, week after week, the effortless prose of E. B. White and James Thurber.

Writing is hard enough without having to see those who are so good at it make it look so easy.

I am indebted to both, however, for the inspiration they gave me, by example.

Thurber fashioned a model of sorts in his book *The Years With Ross* (Atlantic-Little, Brown). He told how the editor of *The New Yorker*, Harold Ross, managed to create a coherent strategy and character for the magazine in spite of constant, complex business problems. GE management did the same, on a grander scale. In both cases, spirited people brightened the scene.

E. B. White fashioned the form for insightful, graceful prose. I've never read a word of his that didn't fit the mold. Any writer who came from a farm area like Iowa, where I grew up, will recognize in an instant what White meant when he wrote to Thurber in 1938: "I don't know which is more discouraging, literature or chickens."

Encouragement for this book did come from several close associates from the days at GE Corporate Marketing. Heading the list is John Duncan, a master of gentle persuasion, along with Roy Stratton, Bill Berg, Bill Hickman, and Nat Boynton. I've been urged on by another ex-A&SPer, Dale Strand, who MC's the GE Alumni Club meetings every other year in New York City.

I'm grateful for the book design by Deborah Keats, who was an A&SP art director as the GE story unfolded in later years, and who now runs her own studio – Keats, design – in Schenectady. Composition was handled by Ben Fuina, a friend who served a lot of us at GE for many years as the head of his own firm, Word Management, in Albany, NY. Final polishing came from Pewilla Dick, who honed her editing skills at Little, Brown & Company.

This book, of course, would never have come about without the enduring understanding and support of my wife, Elizabeth, a talented writer on her own. And I gained quizzical support, if not understanding, from our four children as they came and went, wondering all the while what their father was doing hunched up at his computer down in the study.

J.R.B.

I

FAMILY TIES

"I think I have the answer to your problem," said ex-A&SPer Carleton J. Hawthorne as he was introduced to the gathered members of the agency. Corkey then proceeded to outline, without attribution, the most popular direct mail program ever produced by his alma mater. "We'll call it," he mused, with a profound glance at the ceiling, "Hidden Values." The eyes of the principals bulged with the message: "Marketing magic."

In 1985, the marketing and sales organizations of GE were supported by 127 different advertising components.

Each, with the exception of one, had its own ad manager and budget to promote the virtues of its products and services. These were GE clients.

Then there was the 127th component – an advertising agency. It was never lumped in with the 36 agencies of record from outside the company which served GE clients, let alone the legion of others which skirmished on the fringes of GE ad budgets.

The component was the Advertising and Sales Promotion Department. It was a kind of super agency, inside the company and in the know, serving more GE segments than all the outsiders put together. A&SP was a major source for GE client businesses looking for management talent, and a favorite raiding ground for outside agencies and advertisers looking for manpower and inspiration.

In the eyes of a good many of those who began their careers with the company, A&SP was at the heart of the marketing and sales action at GE. Certainly A&SP people were at the fulcrum of company-wide communications.

A GE profile

A glance at the profile of the typical GE advertising professional will show you why. The portrait was sketched by the GE Corporate Communications Council in 1979 when it met at the Doral in Miami.

The average age of the 142 conferees was 42.3 years. The youngest was 25, the oldest 63. Each had been with GE 16.8 years, on average, starting at age 26. Ten of the group were females including, according to GE standards, the youngster of 25.

The typical attendee had held five GE positions; five of those at the conference had passed through 15 or more jobs. Seventy brought outside experience into the company. A third of the total had communications degrees, with 15% in advertising. Five per cent held MBAs.

Four of every 10 conferees were graduates of A&SP's Advertising and Public Relations (APR) training program.

The printed agenda, incidentally, included one biography familiar to anyone who had ever been a member of A&SP – Gregory Ellis (i.e., GE), the "Manager of Distributive Processing, Analysis and Salutations." This ghostly appellation signed off on countless GE mailings, and was one reason why the U.S. Postal Service gave GE in Schenectady the Zip Code 12345. The agenda noted: "Currently, Mr. Ellis is working on reducing the 50 state abbreviations to one letter each."

Sibling rivalry

Not all GE people would agree that A&SP had a lock on GE communications. Within the family, there was a certain amount of sibling rivalry.

In some GE growth areas, like plastics, the feeling toward A&SP was akin to that of the upstart younger brother: You're not with it, Gramps.

In the GE consumer goods world, it was more like that of the sister to a younger brother: You don't understand women, honey, so get lost.

Some who left the company retained a kind of love-hate relationship. Bill McGuckin, former ad manager for GE computers, sent greetings from Phoenix: "Hope all goes well for everyone in Schenectigrad." Dick Elsberry, who was "frosted" when

A&SP released him after 30 years, at the same time as nearly everyone else, told of his relish for freelancing in one of his first major pieces, "Set Free," in *The New York Times Magazine.* His subject? A&SP.

Other alumni were just plain disdainful. *Dun's Review* quoted one, a few years back: "The guys I know who are still there have pretty good salaries and awfully big offices, but they have 'nothing' jobs."

Not so, said ex-A&SPer Bob Fegley, who wound up as staff executive and speech writer for GE CEOs Fred Borch and Reg Jones. Before his retirement, Bob noted: "This company is taking some business risks that would stand your hair on end ... There are days – or months – when the glamour wears pretty thin, and some disappointments are inevitable. But there are other days – and those are the ones that count – when something works out, and you know that you have your hands on the levers that move the world."

Certainly, A&SP had the tools to do it. It developed capabilities that went far beyond what any other agency could field. Need an exhibit? A market development program? A handbook? A video show? A technical bulletin? A brochure? A sales incentive program? A training aid? A hot air balloon? A&SP would produce any or all of them, as it had so many times before.

And, oh yes, A&SP would handle your advertising, too.

The company you keep

GE people who needed those tools viewed A&SP as pretty good company, for a number of reasons.

Some preferred A&SP because they knew they wouldn't have to start from square one explaining how GE works. Others knew that A&SP did a lot for the corporate executive office, and therefore assumed it was a safe place to do business. Marketing and general managers, more and more, came from the engineering and financial disciplines and thus turned to A&SP to fill in the marketing and sales promotion potholes in their career paths.

Many GE ad managers simply liked to deal with their old buddies in A&SP. Still others used A&SP because of inertia: it would take on anything you wanted, including a good share of your own job, and produce a reasonable return for your money.

The summary judgment of GE people was that A&SP was an agency you could feel comfortable with ... an outfit which had been around as long as anyone could remember.

A&SP had, literally, been around as long as the General Electric Company. Tom Edison was really the first A&SPer, tapping out word of his inventions on a Western Union telegraph key installed in his office.

The metamorphosis

A fascinating metamorphosis began when A&SP was organized to produce publications in 1893, a year after the company was founded. From that informational base, it mushroomed into a large, tightly knit, centrally controlled marketing and promotional powerhouse, offering every imaginable service. By the early '60s, A&SP's general manager even headed the company's radio and TV stations in Schenectady, along with a multi-million dollar GE printing firm.

In 1952, when GE was decentralized, A&SP took on the true competitive stance of an agency, shifting to profit and loss. It strengthened its position throughout the company, and expanded even further in the '60s and early '70s.

A&SP opened five branch offices from coast to coast. It leapfrogged to Europe with a four-nation network in support of GE international businesses. It made an abortive fling at accounts outside of GE. On a competitive basis, it secured all of the product PR business in the company. This was no small feat in the face of formidable big timers like Young & Rubicam, which already handled a large chunk of GE consumer communications, plus the fact – as anyone who's worked both sides of the street knows – that it's much more difficult to sell from inside a company than from the outside.

The inevitable pull-back began in the mid-1970s. A&SP regrouped in two locations, in and around Schenectady, and in Connecticut. It forged an organizational link with GE corporate, first through public relations, then marketing.

As a part of the usual soul-searching, there came the uneasy realization that agencies are a dime a dozen, and that GE can buy whatever it needs on the outside. A&SP was greatly scaled down; the emphasis shifted more from doing to thinking – essentially marketing and sales strategy and program planning. The shrunken core of consultants that remained in 1987 was a far cry from the crowds and glory.

In the midst of all that churning, there were people – people coming and going, some leaving for good, some coming back. But among those who left GE with finality for the other world, the view of A&SP was maybe not so fraternal, as with GE clients, but maternal. As you might expect between parent and child, there was a fair amount of give and take.

The giving was mostly in the talent and differing viewpoints brought by those who joined A&SP from all over the country. The take-away came about when they left, transporting great amounts of skills, borrowed ideas, and friendship. Sighed Lord Einstein's Bob Wells: "If only someone could have bottled all the talent that drifted through the halls of Building 22; or was it 6?"

The New York Times quoted ex-A&SPer Carl Ally as saying: "I learned all my fundamentals at General Electric. I haven't had to learn anything else since." In the same article, reporting on a GE Alumni Club meeting, Master of Ceremonies Dale Strand, at the time a vice president of Ticketron, and now president of Bedford/Comstock Ltd. in Stamford, CT added: "They taught us to be thorough professionals in every conceivable area of communication. They taught us that the diamond is multi-faceted."

Sharing "Values"

Corkey Hawthorne, noted above, wasn't the first to borrow the marketing theme of Hidden Values. Another alumnus received a $1,000 bonus from a top New York City agency for "his idea." It was also used within A&SP by half a dozen others, including me, and claimed as the prodigy of at least three originators. Fortunately, there was never any conflict among recipients as long as the markets were different. Which, within GE, was easy.

The program worked best with a commodity product where subtle advantages weren't readily apparent. Each mailer highlighted one such difference and related it to an affixed item, such as an old coin or stamp.

The gimmick was that while the value of most items was nominal, one of every 25 was really valuable. The only way to find out was to call the GE sales engineer who had a record of the numbered, winning mailers – ergo, the prospect opened his or her own door for a sales call. Beautiful.

The list of items used was lengthy – gem stones, arrowheads, fool's gold vs. real nuggets, Indian head pennies, Columbian commemorative U.S. stamps, and so on. The program was always a roaring success with everyone, except for the poor soul at the bottom of the A&SP heap who had to administer it and keep track of the valuables.

The give and take seemed endless, extending beyond GE to A&SP alumni. Gerber's Tom Hougan recalls a learning experience as an APR trainee in Schenectady:

"Merle Bonthuis made me write a switchgear job 40 times." Then, says Tom with chagrin, "he found the lead in the fourth paragraph." Bonthuis still shepherds the company's new Corporate Identity Program on the staff of GE Corporate Marketing & Sales in Fairfield.

Ties that bond

A visitor to an exhibit conference in 1985 told ex-A&SPer John Stoutland "The biggest problem working with your alumni is the bonding ritual. You people talk among yourselves for half an hour before getting down to business." John, who recently retired as marketing communications manager for GE motors in Ft. Wayne, noted simply: "I was a member of the Class of '53."

John Kolody, who heads his own advertising and PR firm in Ossining, NY, muses: "It's interesting that A&SP maintains its hold on us – more than college, more than any other past relationship." Bill Lewellen, now president of Maritz Marketing Research in St. Louis, adds: "I've had just two employers and I've been proud of the progress of both."

As a result, ex-A&SPers tend to emulate their alma mater in differing ways. Many, as noted, started their own agencies.

Others beefed up advertising staffs in the image of A&SP. When Glen Peterson left as ad manager of GE instruments to become director of corporate communications at Foxboro, he promptly installed a 225-person staff to launch communications from in-house.

Others looked to A&SP for staffers. Frank O'Keefe, for example, left A&SP to transform Armstrong Rubber into Armtek, triple its sales to $1 billion, then sell it in a leveraged buyout in 1988 for $650 million. In the doing, he brought in ex-A&SPer Bob Jones to head up corporate communications; Bill Troy, who ran the GE House of Magic, as his vice president of sales; and contracted for free lancing from ex-A&SPer Lou Marsh along with, for his annual report, the man who put out the same for GE, Hervie Haufler.

GE ad managers still turn to ex-A&SPers to handle their accounts. "I miss the old days," says Tom McLaren, ad manager for GE meters in Somersworth, NH. But his yearning has been assuaged by service from the Doremus agency out of Boston – by account execs and ex-A&SPers Garrett Sheahan, until his recent death, and now by Alan Griffin.

Sweet talk

One A&SP alumnus, Tom Berquist, started a different kind of idea factory. His Pre-emptive Products Inc., in Stratford, CT specializes in developing kiddy candy. Tom's first big hit is Boogers, a gummy candy which . . . but that's probably more than you want to know.

A&SP's presence in the business world is pervasive. A few years ago, a single issue of *Industrial Marketing* carried word of three alumni: Carl Bahn, named manager of advertising and PR for Riley Stoker; Bob Singer, with an article expressing his view as a space rep, "Advertising Consistency and Your Bottom Line"; and a Perspectives piece by Jim DeWeese, now deceased but then head of Wolff Associates in Rochester, NY and a former president of the Business/Professional Advertising Association.

A 1985 A.N.A. management conference featured four ex-A&SPers: Bob Lauterborn, then corporate advertising head of International Paper (now professor of journalism at the University of North Carolina); Bart Snider and Dick Huether, with GE Corporate Marketing; and John Zeeman, executive vice president of marketing and planning, United Airlines.

A&SPers even seem intent on infiltrating the competitors they jousted with while at GE. Tom Keller is vice president of corporate communications for Siemens, along with associates Kevin Kimball and Tom Varney, while Rod Sipe, aided by Debbie Hoyt, handles marketing communications for OSRAM, a Siemens subsidiary. In the opposite corner is Pat Wilson, lobbing releases for the U.S. consumer electronics arm of the giant Dutch firm, Philips.

Club news

There's a ground swell of interest in GE alumni clubs beyond the one in New York City. Schenectady has one that's met a couple of times yearly since the department's major breakup in 1985. Free lancer Joan A'Hearn, who was a favorite script writer for top GE executives while with A&SP, reports on efforts in Connecticut "to start a similar group . . . from the almost bottomless well of ex-GE types who live and work in Fairfield County." From Chicago comes the plaintive cry of Hank Hamblin, CEO of Russell Hampton Co., which turns out all of the paraphernalia for service clubs such as Rotary: "Why not hold a Chicago bash for us Midwestern shut-ins?"

A&SPers even have their own newsletter which comes out on an irregular basis from Light & Power Productions, home to several ex-A&SPers, in Scotia, NY, a Schenectady suburb. Art Dwyer, CEO of Atlanta-based Communication Trends which created both the marketing plan and launch campaign for Ted

Turner's CNN and TNT, retorts: "I like the newsletter better than my college alumni paper."

Glenn Storino, now a managing partner of Atlanta's Brush Creek Consulting Group writes: "How absolutely delightful to receive my copy . . . Times were simpler then . . . happier. We were all on our way somewhere which only the future could define."

All in the family

The developing family relationships seem at times to border on incest. *The Wall Street Journal* reported one instance in a front page story a few years back.

Monsanto launched a promotional program for Lasso, a herbicide made in St. Louis, and the paper quoted Michael Rohan, ad manager for the firm's agricultural products. Mike is an A&SP alumnus.

The *Journal* also quoted John Jordan, president of Lasso's agency, now Muller Jordan Weiss of New York City. As already noted, Jordan and Muller are A&SP alumni.

While the article didn't say so, Monsanto's corporate account was handled by another New York agency, Trout and Ries. Jack Trout, the president who handled the account, and Al Ries, the agency chairman, both started with A&SP.

It wasn't long thereafter that Monsanto asked Trout and Ries to put together an industry-wide program that would present to the public the good side of chemicals. This, it was hoped, would counteract some of the things people were beginning to say about the bad side.

One of the first things Jack did was to get in touch with A&SP, because he knew we had put together a couple of similar GE market development programs. A&SP's GM at the time, Bob Pulver, referred Jack to me, since I had worked on both. One was Live Better . . . Electrically, a massive industry-wide effort to get people to use more electrical appliances in the home. The other, even more pertinent, was Citizen Atom, which was designed to counteract the public's nervousness about nuclear power.

Now, none of this is meant to say that GE had all the answers. But it does tell you a couple of things.

One is that whatever the communication task to be done, it was a pretty safe bet that A&SP had already tested the water.

And two, wherever you are now, it's very likely there's an ex-A&SPer nearby who with one phone call can maybe save you from re-inventing the wheel.

If you were once a part of the A&SP family within GE, that may not be enough to make you want to go home. But it'll likely make you carry around some fond memories of the time spent with mother.

II
CLASS ACT

The young man from the GE news bureau had been invited to speak to my creative writing class at the YWCA on "How I write." After talking no more than three minutes, he sat down, leaving me to fill up the remaining two hours of class time. Hervie Haufler, the GE corporate editor who had brought him to class, shrugged: "Kurt Vonnegut doesn't talk much, but he sure knows how to write."

Young people who wanted to enter the world of big business in the early part of the last half century found GE to be a tempting doorway.

On-the-job training brought schooling in a dozen disciplines – technical marketing, financial management, engineering, manufacturing, etc. In the late '40s, GE added a brand new entry, the Advertising Training Course.

Most college grads who had the choice opted for A&SP over other ad agencies – even the big ones on Madison Avenue – for a couple of good reasons: the pay was better, and GE offered real work instead of a slot in the mail room. The class spirit engendered through that training program, along with close personal links forged at work and at play, still bind A&SP alumni to their alma mater and to each other.

Prototype '48

The doings of the class of 1948, of which I was a member, formed the prototype for those which followed over the next three decades. There were 39 of us, coming from 13 states as graduates of everything from state universities and Ivy League schools to large and small colleges and universities, from coast to coast.

A degree was the price of admission; it was assumed you had talent. Even so, the first work assignment for each was due as much to the whims of those who had been in charge since before the war, as to any latent potential.

The usual procedure was for recruits, one by one, to parade before management, then await the Word.

The future executive vice president of Muller Jordan Weiss, Frank Muller, just out of Tufts, was assigned to the instruction book section, which trainees soon concluded was A&SP's equivalent of Siberia. Others were scattered throughout the exhibit operation, the art department, the visual education section, the news bureau, and so on.

Some with technical degrees got "test" assignments which placed them side by side with engineers in GE manufacturing plants. Others were assigned to the marketing sections of product departments. Three wound up in Boston, New York City and Atlanta generating customer promotion for district salesmen. Three more stayed at A&SP headquarters in Schenectady lending sales support to their district A&SP compatriots in the field.

The future CEO of Ally & Gargano, fresh from the University of Michigan, started off in the printing section. Carl noted later, from the perspective of Madison Avenue: "I learned certain fundamental things which I now find shockingly absent in many of the people who come to work in our place. The routine tools of the trade were presented to me in an orderly fashion, and I had the experience of this very purposeful kind of introduction to the advertising business, for which I'm deeply grateful."

The future president of GE Mexico, and later president of Bulova Watch Co. (Ken Yarbrough, Iowa State), went to work as an administrative clerk.

The luck of the draw ran out for George Cahaney from Notre Dame. He discovered that A&SP did indeed have a version of the mail room, called Distribution. However, this was no ordinary mail room. In fact, even the most mundane of A&SP assignments ushered newcomers into the GE arena of big business.

Every year, A&SP typically produced 300 new promotional brochures. A&SP also prepared close to a thousand instruction manuals, ranging from a simple hang tag for a $2 insulator to a 20 volume set of five-inch-thick books probing a multi-million dollar power system that covered 10 acres. And, yearly, A&SP produced 3,000 new or revised handbook pages, totalling as many as nine million printed sheets, to update the 27,000 customer handbooks on its distribution list.

Since A&SP produced several million copies of publications every year, it also had its own four-story printing plant called the Maqua Company, a wholly owned GE subsidiary. (Maqua was the name given the local Indians by the Dutch who settled the area; later, the French called them the Iroquois.)

Down in the mail room, a million and a half mailers went out each year, while 150,000 shipments each week responded to customer inquiries. The inquiries in themselves were an education.

"This is God calling"

From out of the blue: "Would you be interested in selling your company?" (No.) "Can you please send God some information on the TeleVideo system?" (O.K. This was from Y. E. God, owner of the Kingdom of God company, York, PA.) "Would you please send a publication on every product GE makes?" (Sure. Send around a boxcar to our warehouse in Scotia, and we'll send you a copy of each of the 40,000 stocked there.) From Sears: "Mr. and Mrs. G. Electric are invited to apply for credit." (Many thanks.)

A select number in the class of '48 got to do what everyone really wanted to do: write ad copy. The chosen few included the future presidents of Ross Roy N.Y. (Hank Larson, Columbia) and of Muller Jordan Weiss (John Jordan, DePauw), and me (University of Iowa).

My selection came as a double ploy. Since I had filled creative as well as account assignments at Bozell & Jacobs in Omaha during and after college, I bundled up a big box of samples for review by the A&SP brass – marketing plans, ads, brochures, house organs, scripts for three weekly radio shows, ghost writing for Father Flanagan at nearby Boys Town, along with newspaper work from my Stars & Stripes duty in the Far East, following a free tour of the South Pacific as a combat infantryman. The sheer bulk must have been intimidating.

Then during the interview in Schenectady, when the head of technical publications, Warren O'Neal, asked if I would like to work for him, I gave the answer which for a job applicant in that era was almost unthinkable: "No." Whatever the reasons, John was sent to industrial advertising, Hank to the group promoting GE transportation products, and I to the team which handled the wire and cable as well as lighting and rectifier accounts.

On-the-job training

It is literally true that every GE trainee begins useful work the first day. In my case, there was only an hour's delay while a long term A&SP veteran named Lou Albee patiently answered my question: "What's the difference between ac and dc power?"

The first assignment was typical of many trainees: I was to prepare a communications plan to introduce a new product for the rectifier business, the Battery Vitalizer. This was designed to hang from the steering wheel of a car, with one lead plugged into the cigarette lighter and the other into the power outlet of a garage. It promised quick starts in even the coldest weather because the car's battery was constantly re-charged overnight. I asked the obvious question: What about the Sun Belt states – roughly half the market – where nobody worries about cold weather? And a couple of research sorties revealed that not many people up north at that time had garages wired for electricity. After a brief flurry of test market promotion, the project was cancelled.

By helping kill the Battery Vitalizer project, A&SP served the marketing interests of the client as much as it did the credibility of the agency. A&SP was in the unique position where it could identify with both.

The Battery Vitalizer wasn't the sole product dreamed up by GE engineers in isolation, only to founder when people didn't line up to buy. Another was the electric Cattle Stock Tank De-Icer, which did just what it says, and ditto for the electric Calf De-Horner.

Yet another was the Electrall, a farm tractor system which worked like a miniature version of the power unit for a diesel-electric locomotive. The Electrall's engine turned a generator, and the electricity from that operated plows and other power take-off equipment. The design was fine . . . but it was so complicated and expensive that farmers flocked the other way.

An A&SP art director, Merrill Shook, discovered a unique product looking for a market, this time in the sink of the home he bought from a GE engineer.

The "Electric Pig"

The former owner and inventor called his device the "Electric Pig" because, as he put it, "it eats garbage." It may well have remained a kitchen curiosity, if it had not been for an astute GE marketer who recognized the appeal for homemakers, renamed it the Disposall, and created a brand new business for GE.

While not everyone got the first A&SP assignment desired, the alternative was bearable for a couple of reasons. One: a different, probably better job was bound to come through "rotation."

This was based on the precept that if one were to conduct the full symphony of A&SP communication instruments, then one had better learn how to play the piccolo and bass drum along with the strings. After learning a succession of skills while rotating through a succession of jobs, one might in four or five years, if one were lucky, become – voila! – an account supervisor. That is today's equivalent of account executive in the typical agency.

"How-to" lessons

The other thing that made a dull job bearable was the intermingling with one's peers in weekly A&SP classes. These were, in effect, "how to" courses that taught everything about every instrument in the A&SP orchestra: copywriting, news writing, film making, distribution, media, marketing strategy, sales techniques, program planning, accounting, printing, production, exhibits, graphics, catalogs, direct mail, and so on.

The classes did not merely repeat what one learned in college. It was more like the Army: your old professors may have had *their* way, and other companies undoubtedly had *their* way, but this was the *GE way*.

Everybody in marketing at GE, including A&SP trainees, attended a series of Sales Analysis Institute classes. SAI drilled into us a rudimentary system of sales movers. Customer benefits, for example, were called Plus Ones. Features, which came next in support of benefits, were Plus Twos, and so on. A difficult customer was an Oh-Nine. And no GE alumnus will ever forget a *very* difficult customer – a Revolving Oh-Nine.

A&SP etched its own way, first of all, in a huge binder called the Procedures Manual, outlining every step one might need to take to get anything done. These routines were then elaborated on by class instructors, A&SP pros who maybe didn't know everything about communications, but surely knew how it was done at GE. Their lectures were reinforced by experts from the GE product businesses.

GE bloopers

It was fascinating to learn from the latter that while GE was awfully good about coming up with new products, the company – seemingly through a surfeit of naive arrogance – was not very adept at exploiting them.

In 1924, as one example, GE built the first diesel-electric locomotive. Then, according to the people from the GE plant in Erie, Pennsylvania, the engineer who dreamed it up became disillusioned at the lack of support for it, and went off to General Motors. GM promptly exploited the enormous potential, and dominated the market for decades. GE also built the first U.S. jet engine in the early 1940s, based on the Whittle design brought over from England during the war, but saw a promising commercial advantage slip away to Pratt & Whitney. It was not until the 1980s that GE clawed its way back to a strong position in both markets.

Most A&SP trainees coming out of college had one thing in common – they were broke. So they supplemented their GE salaries with outside jobs, mostly related to work. Carl Ally, for example, sold encyclopedias door to door where he found it easiest – "in the toughest part of town."

Others free-lanced with local agencies. One of my ventures was the YWCA creative writing class, where Kurt Vonnegut lectured, after a fashion. Hervie Haufler did his best to get Kurt on a roll: "That was an interesting narrative technique you used in the story." To which Kurt responded: "Is *that* what it was?" To this day, Hervie isn't sure if it were on the level, or just a put-on by Kurt so no one would ask him again to do something he obviously disliked.

Avon calling

One of the lecturers in our marketing class was a young man named Hicks Waldron, who later left his position at GE as vice president and group executive of consumer products to become CEO of Standard Brands and then Avon Products. He told us of a GE vice president who invested huge sums to produce the perfect automotive starter. It actually was, but it also cost twice as much to produce as penny-conscious Detroit would consider.

A key part of A&SP class routine was homework, the planning and producing of actual pieces based on real world problems. In the final session of the program planning course, each class prepared and proposed an integrated campaign to the marketing and sales managers of a product component. Some ideas, like the ad to promote industrial motors in *The New Yorker,* never sold, but other fresh viewpoints did make it to print.

After a specified number of years – usually two – and a specified number of courses – usually eight to 10 – A&SP trainees were graduated with ceremonies and certificates. It sounds corny now, but up through the 1960s, it made a difference: it was much easier to get gigs around the company if you were a full fledged member of the orchestra.

Throughout the whirl of schooling and job changes, the class of '48 was acutely aware of one constant – A&SP's general manager, J. Stanford Smith.

Stan was a hefty man whose suits fought a losing battle with his waistline. The flopping fabrics went unnoticed, however, as we watched him spew ideas in ebullient abandon.

Stan Smith, conductor

Stan's presence was pervasive. This general manager was not just concerned with the full symphonic sound. He wanted to hear each person perform separately. And did.

Stan sent you a note if he liked your work. He sent you a note if he did not like your work. Either way, you knew that he knew what you were doing, that he read every word you wrote.

He had a flair for the dramatic. Stan kept looking for new ways to impart his feelings and philosophy.

"GE doesn't *try* to do good," he would boom. "We *strive* to do good!" Then Smith went on, somewhat incongruously, "We're not going to do an attitude survey in Brooklyn, New York. We're going to do it in Horseheads, New York. I want people to remember what we do, and what we say!"

In short, Stan felt that if General Electric were to be viewed as a leader, it must look, act, and speak like one.

He strongly expressed this view, too, in work reviews. He presided over formal ones every Monday morning in Planning Board; informal ones went on all the time in his office. To make a point in the former, he once threw comp layouts on the floor and stomped on them. "These are all wrong," he roared, then proceeded to tell us why.

Another time, in his office, he solemnly picked up some layouts under review, walked to the window, and dropped them out. Turning, he asked: "Do you want to know what I think about them?"

"Pat and Goose"

What he usually thought was that we had failed to follow the "Pat and Goose" school of advertising. This was his view of what any ad beyond a pure product ad should do: let a recognized leader (GE) show an unknown (any customer) how it could become a leader, too. "We'll do what they all want," he hammered away: "Make 'em rich and famous!"

John Jordan used Smith's formula to fashion a new campaign for GE's power equipment business. The ads didn't just say that GE built good turbines. The head shouted "Engineering enterprise and financial daring!" The copy, then, in persuasive terms related how GE had undertaken a long and costly journey to come up with a radically new turbine design – which incidentally had a price tag of $30 million. But GE did it, as reported in the ad, and the featured customer had extraordinary foresight in buying it, because homeowners would surely need more electricity a few years down the road.

This was classic Smith, classic "Pat and Goose." Publicly pat the customer on the back for acting like a leader, but at the same time goose him subtly to keep at it (buy more turbines) so people would know the customer really *was* a leader.

The benevolent despot

In other ways, Smith was almost a father figure. One time, exasperated that so many trainees had left the plant for coffee at the nearby Tick Tock diner, Smith stormed across the street, clambered on top of a table, and ordered everyone to get back to work.

While he was a tough taskmaster, Smith was also benevolent. He welcomed each incoming class with a formal luncheon. Trainees were invited as a group to attend A&SP business reviews at nearby resorts, like the Gideon Putnam in Saratoga Springs, where one could usually hobnob in the bar with actor Monty Woolley. Stan often visited in the classroom and spoke at each graduation, insisting on group pictures.

Smith also invited trainees to his camp at Lake George for games and a corn roast – an evocation of his home state, Indiana. He also solicited help from trainees to put in the dock and touch up his cabin.

It was not unusual, either, for him to show up at your door with flowers and fruit for a sick child or spouse. At one time or another, at least in his early days as general manager, most of us young trainees and wives were invited for dinner around the kitchen table of his home in suburban Scotia.

All the while, he was praising, analyzing, exhorting, encouraging, inspiring. With Smith, things were never dull, never quiet, never half way.

In between, trainees found other matters of interest in Schenectady. Most things interacted with General Electric, which was an entity unto itself, at one point employing more than 40,000 people in a city not even twice that big.

There were company Field Days at the Edison Club, originally a country club solely for GE employees. (One A&SP trainee, Jerry Olive, is the only person on record there to have lost a ball while putting.) There was the GEAA, a company athletic association which had a health club facility within the plant as big as many factory bays. And there were Triple A (Apparatus Advertising Association) athletic teams sponsored by A&SP. An ex-A&SPer who's now editor of *Cogeneration* magazine in Washington, DC, Earl Dunckel, recently showed up with a newspaper clipping of an A&SP baseball team; he had kept the snippet in his wallet for more than 30 years.

Digging for gems

For a long time, A&SP also maintained an extensive advertising library that was a treasure of experience for the digging. This was B.O. (Before Ogilvy), but it put trainees on reading terms with such early practicioners as Clyde Bedell, Earnest Elmo Calkins, James Webb Young, and John Caples, all of whom explored and exploited human feelings and failings.

The library disclosed that we were among distinguished company. Charles Lamb, Aldous Huxley, Lord Byron, Bernard Shaw, John P. Marquand, Sherwood Anderson, William Faulkner, Christopher Morley – all tried their hand at writing ads before going on to other careers.

A&SPers were served good advice, too, from stylists such as E. B. White. In one of the slimmest, but most fertile, library volumes, *The Elements of Style,* he loosened our leash a notch: "Never imitate consciously, but do not worry about being an imitator; take pains instead to admire what is good. Then when you write in a way that comes naturally, you will echo the halloos that bear repeating."

Ah, yes, Schenectady

And then, for trainees, there was Schenectady. Ah yes, Schenectady.

It wasn't for everybody. In 1952, a young A&SP recruit from Texas got off the train in the middle of town in the middle of winter. He walked a half block to the corner, peered into the biting wind coming up from the GE plant at the end of Erie

Boulevard, and promptly got back on the train to go home. He never said why.

A few years later, Joe Morton of A&SP's news bureau prepared an "Eating and Restaurant Guide for Schenectady, New York", for GE PR people gathering from all parts of the country. It included Ecobelli's Tam O' Shanter ("Fillet O'Mignon a specialty"), Sleasman's Hofbrau ("Chef speaks German with a French accent. Tres Chic. Chic tends bar"), and the White Tower ("Feeds 800 people eight at a time").

These were all for real, all in Schenectady.

He could have set in boldface LeRoy's Chicken Shack, which was well known if not well patronized by A&SP. Instead, Joe honored the last restaurant on the list with a star: Voison, 150 miles away at 575 Park Avenue in New York City. Concluded Joe: "A long drive, but well worth it."

Schenectady takes a lot of ribbing, but it's often tinged with nostalgia. Ex-A&SPer Zane Robbins recently wrote: "If I ever get a half way decent excuse to visit upstate New York, you can be sure I'll look in on A&SP . . . if I can find the damned place."

The goodbye

Eventually, without any great fanfare, class was over for A&SP newcomers. It wasn't the graduation ceremony and it didn't happen on any particular day. But each class knew that something special had ended, and that things would never be quite the same.

Of those who came in 1948, Carl packed his trailer and headed west, although he wasn't sure where he was going. Frank and John and Hank headed south to try their luck in the big city. Jack left to try teaching at the University of Oregon. Chuck flew off as an airline pilot. And although we never knew for sure, everyone assumed that Sherm Stone would parlay the routines he developed at the old McLane Hotel along the Mohawk at Rexford onto the stand-up comic circuit. The rest of us went our own ways, one by one, year by year.

What is left of the classes over the following 40 years is largely memories. In fact, that is all that's left of the Advertising and Public Relations (APR) training program, as it was known when it began tailing off in the 1970s.

As much as anything else, the demise stemmed from the Protest Movement in the '60s. Newcomers to A&SP complained that the courses repeated what they had already learned in college and were, therefore, a waste of time. The feeling was: forget the past, and forget the details. Show us the big picture and let us do our own thing.

Management figured maybe they were right. So in the early part of the '70s, A&SP brought in a group of outside consultants to replace all of the previous A&SP courses with a single one called MCP – the Marketing Communications Program.

Successor to APR: MCP

Instead of exploring a myriad of marketing, sales and advertising situations, as had been done before, MCP focused on a single case history: a 12-months' span when the fictional Merton Electronics Company struggled to expand from an OEM making chips to a company introducing calculators into the highly competitive consumer market.

Integrated instruction modules took A&SPers from product concept through market acceptance, following four viewpoints – marketing management, advertising management, account management, and creative direction.

Classes were held in various A&SP locations over a period of 15 years. Recruiting was at a low level, so older hands mixed in with newcomers to swell the rosters. After a switch came in 1981 from college recruiting to professional hires, A&SP cancelled MCP and the formal training program sputtered to a halt.

A&SP never did make a definitive judgment on MCP, except to conclude that it was a unique concept. Certainly it was in scope, even though the original five volumes of instructional materials were boiled down from 4,000 pages to half that number.

That in itself prompts speculation. The Limited Edition Club's seven volumes of Edward Gibbon's *The Decline and Fall of The Roman Empire*, set in 11 pt. Garamond and illustrated with the etchings of Piranesi, total only 2,538 pages. One wonders if this wouldn't have been just as useful as a substitute, adding a mere four hundred pages but enriching readers with every human foible, spanning 1400 eventful years instead of just one.

It remains to be seen if the volumes from MCP or earlier A&SP training programs will long survive, let alone – in the manner of Gibbon – "ever be remembered."

III

GHOST STORIES

As the vice president of GE Apparatus Sales read from my script for "The City of Tomorrow," by mistake he turned four pages at once. Imperturbably, he read on as A&SP's Doug Crossman frantically shifted slides to catch up. Nobody noticed, which was either a tribute to Pat O'Brien's skills as a speaker, or an indictment of my gifts as a speechwriter.

The changing role of GE marketing, year on year, dictated for A&SP the services it should add, nurture or drop. But there was never any question that one function was inviolable: audio visual communications, or as A&SP called it, AVCOM.

After all, as one wag put it, this was not a matter of being on hand to help a lieutenant make a speech, or a major, or even a colonel. A&SP was there to prop up *General* Electric.

Propping up the General

Ghosting speeches, of course, was only part of the voice lessons. AVCOM specialists, over the course of A&SP's history, pumped out a torrent of movies, videotapes, multi-image shows, stage presentations, exhibits, road shows, executive conferences, slide talks, educational programs, point of purchase displays, and so on.

While no one year could be called typical, AVCOM in 1976 had the lead role for eight high level company meetings, including three at corporate, handled the writing and visualizing of speeches for the chairman and several hundred other top executives, including 20 vice presidents, completed seven motion pictures and several 12-projector multi-image shows, produced more than 10,000 slides (not counting those made on GE-designed, computerized Genigraphics equipment), and spear-headed GE shows in seven foreign countries.

To produce this kind of volume, A&SP had in place, at various points in time, project supervisors, writers and visualizers, film and video directors, cinematographers, film editors, motion picture production specialists with lab facilities, and exhibit coordinators backed up by a shop complete with cabinetmakers, painters and electricians.

A&SP, in the guise of AVCOM, literally was ready to take on anything that was supposed to speak or move.

The posture on projects was uncomplicated. "People want high quality, low cost, and a short time schedule," said AVCOM's Ray Bonta. "They can have any two, but not all three at the same time."

Wooing Jersey Central

Some AVCOM projects were so elaborate the medium got in the way of the message. A presentation to Jersey Central Power & Light in 1962 made this clear.

For the better part of a decade, GE had played a strong lead in developing the market for atomic power plants. But no utility had been willing to invest $80 million to put up the first full-scale facility. GE's traditional role had been to provide just the nuclear reactor and steam turbine, while the utility contracted separately for the boiler, buildings and other equipment.

Finally, in a mixture of desperation and exasperation, GE decided to offer the whole plant at an attractive firm price – a turnkey bargain. Jersey Central was the target prospect, with its chairman the audience of one.

To dramatize the story, A&SP built a monstrous but portable display unit, complete with built-in rear screen projectors, automatic drapes, motorized podium, and a dazzling array of lights and sound. Today, the unit would easily top a quarter of a million dollars.

The effect of the presentation, at least, was electric. Said the utility chairman: "I don't know about the power plant, but the display is terrific! How much do you want for it?" This wasn't exactly what GE had in mind. But later on the utility reconsidered, signed up for the plant, and a business arena blossomed for GE.

Market development: More Power to America

Market development of this kind had been a strong suit of General Electric since its early years. Invariably, A&SP was in the thick of things, with AVCOM playing a lead role. The More Power to America program was a prime example.

GE announced the MPA program to the utility industry in 1945, right after the end of World War II. The proposition was compelling.

The huge consumer demand that had been bottled up during the war years began to fizz. Said GE to its utility friends, "Let's go to our common customers with this message: 'The horse and buggy days are over. Whatever you make or provide, do it electrically.' "

The single goal was the electrification of industry. Specifically, MPA set out to boost U.S. output per manhour by 25 per cent over the rate of growth of the previous 10 years.

The potential pay-off was obvious. Utilities would sell a lot more electricity – their engine of profit. And GE would sell a lot more products, not only to industry but to the utilities, too.

MPA has often been cited as an early example of GE marketing prowess. Its success was due, as much as anything else, to remarkable foresight.

Planning for MPA began in 1942. Keep in mind that this not only was three years before the program was launched but three years before World War II came to an end.

At that time, in fact, not everyone was convinced the war could be won. Britain was besieged. The allies were bogged down in Tunisia, with the invasion of Normandy two years away. The Pacific forces had not yet taken Guadalcanal, the first of the island stepping stones leading to Japan.

Yet back in Schenectady, the planners were busy and confident. They expected not only a favorable end to the war but a consequent boom in business, and they intended to move quickly when it came.

"Make no little plans"

A driving force was Chet Lang, GE's vice president of Apparatus Sales, which served every company market except consumer. His formula for success was simple and direct: "Call, call, call. Sell, sell, sell."

Lang formerly headed the old Publicity Department, the parent organization of A&SP, so it was only natural that he should turn to his communications associates for help. The one he turned to most was Stan Smith, who had been named head of A&SP's AVCOM section in 1944.

Stan liked to quote David Hudson Burnham, a well known architect and city planner: "Make no little plans. They have no magic to stir men's blood." This became Smith's guiding principle for MPA.

The program strategy envisioned four distinct thrusts.

The first seemed mundane, but was crucial to the implementation and success of MPA. GE convinced utilities their 6,000 power salesmen should join GE's sizeable army of sales engineers in promoting electrification to mutual customers. GE also pulled in as allies every conceivable buying influence – consulting engineers, contractors, machinery salesmen, etc. To keep everybody pointed in the right direction, GE published a 28-page monthly magazine called *Load,* which referred to the demand on utilities for electricity.

The 10-car MPA exhibit train

Once these forces were mobilized, A&SP made its second major move, rolling out a 10-car railroad exhibit train crammed with GE products ranging from tiny delicate instruments to working models of huge steel mill drive systems. Even the railway cars were lighted and air conditioned by power from new GE undercarriage systems, while the train itself was pulled by an Alco/GE diesel-electric locomotive.

Because the MPA Special was the first of its kind, there were no guidelines. So A&SP developed its own. Before placing an order for the railroad cars, GE contracted to sell them to the Chicago, Rock Island and Pacific Railroad for conversion to passenger service at the end of the year-long, 30,000-mile tour. A&SP designed the exhibits, coordinated the shipment of the 2,000 GE products to be displayed as well as the construction of car interiors, trained enough GE people to sustain an exhibit manning crew of 20, and mapped out an itinerary covering 150 key U.S. cities.

As a final step, A&SP checked with the people who knew all about this kind of thing: Ringling Brothers-Barnum & Bailey. The latter warned that an advance man should check out every single mile of track and every railroad yard to make sure there were no glitches when the train arrived. The job fell to A&SP's Jack Ewan, who was barely more than a year out of Northwestern. His was one of the more unusual AVCOM assignments of a trainee during any class year.

The MPA train was one of those rare forays where everybody won. GE sales engineers gained a captive audience of 200,000 receptive customers and prospects. The latter saw in one dramatic visit far more than they could ever expect to learn about from a year of GE sales calls. The company gained great credit for leadership from the industry, as well as government and civic leaders. Commendations poured in from such invited guests as Governor Dewey of New York State, the president of MIT, the head of the National Chamber of Commerce, the Secretary of Defense, Henry Ford, and so on.

A&SP was a big winner, too. With the MPA train, it established a reputation throughout GE as the place to go to get the big jobs done. No outside agency had the range of skills needed, or even the interest, to take on and pull off this kind of venture.

Industrial Productivity Forums

A third phase of MPA began concurrently. GE and the utilities hosted Industrial Productivity Forums where the latest in electrification was explored and promoted.

Some programs related only to industries, such as iron and steel, food processing, laundering, or textiles. Others centered on GE products that were of interest to everybody, such as motors and controls, materials handling, and electronic induction heating. Still others aimed at market niches, such as farming.

During the first five years of More Power to America, AVCOM churned out 20 of these programs, producing everything from motion pictures and training courses to displays and literature, along with the meetings where they were used. A&SP account people helped pack the houses with a flood of ads, direct mail, brochures and publicity.

During this period, A&SP sold 150 packaged programs, kept several hundred rental units making the rounds, and through various avenues captured 15 million people for viewings.

The emphasis was heavily canted during the second five years toward subjects of broad public concern, or at least areas where the public should be concerned. GE and its allies recruited local and service groups to show a series of dramatic, A&SP-produced motion pictures, many of which were shown in theatres and on TV: "A Chance to Play" (sports lighting), "Pipeline to the Clouds", (water supplies), "Shining Rails" and "Going Places" (traffic congestion), and "Clean Waters" (pollution control).

The list of subjects was so long and extensive that one AVCOM producer suggested the only meaningful subject not covered was "Clean Poker" – only because, he speculated, it didn't have much sales potential and didn't project the squeaky-clean image that GE wanted.

All of this laid the groundwork for the fourth stage of MPA, and the only one to survive intact much beyond the first decade. This featured Utility Executives conferences – UX, as AVCOM came to call them.

UX at Association Island

Since the utilities were the fulcrum for MPA, A&SP reasoned: let's get their top people together with ours and apply some leverage; we'll report on the great job that's been done, and then show them what needs to be done to keep things rolling.

It was Smith's Pat and Goose all over again, this time in a different form. Which called for AVCOM.

The first question: where to hold the conference? Since there truly had been a long term partnership between GE and utilities, GE chose a place that was steeped in tradition.

That place was Association Island, located a few miles off-shore from Henderson Harbor, NY, on Lake Ontario. GE had owned the place for some time, and used it to bring promising new employees up in the summertime to meet the leaders of GE and to pump them up through a "charge to the rookies." As former Chairman Reg Jones reminisced about his visits there, it was the "one experience that turned us from ordinary people into General Electric people. The monogram was branded indelibly on our souls."

"They should live so long!"

Jones liked to tell how GE President Charlie Wilson, during the early meetings on the Island, scoffed at Westinghouse plans to surpass GE in sales. "They should live so long!" he would roar at the troops in front of Town Hall. "Their grandchildren should live so long!"

Then, related Jones, "He got us out behind the marching band, and they led us out to the flagpole playing 'Onward Christian Soldiers.' At that moment, I would have followed him anywhere on earth – and beyond if necessary."

Charlie Wilson did show up on the last three days during the first UX conference in 1950. This was almost mandatory because the top executives of every major private power company in the U.S. accepted GE's invitation to come to the Island for UX.

But the real driver behind the conference was A&SP. Smith, who had become head of A&SP in 1947, saw to it that his people delved into everything. They were on key committees, prepared and rehearsed the speeches, were assigned to mix with invited customers, and lined up the entertainment, including an opening show with a Broadway cast.

The latter, of course, is no great shakes anymore. But it was, in the context of a time and place when some of the top corporate heads of America came willingly as guests of GE to live in tents, attend reveille and flag raising in the morning, and then in the evening listen to the featured speaker who was the founder of something called the Mobilization of Spiritual Ideals.

At this first UX conference, other vestiges remained of an earlier bond with the audience. Lang reminded his guests of a similar meeting in 1913, when Association Island had been called Camp Cooperation for the occasion. Utility executives heard various talks including one by GE's electrical genius, Charles Proteus Steinmetz, and got a copy of this message from another:

"My wife left for vacation on the 12th. She said I suppose when I am gone it will be the old story, 'When the cat is away the mice will . . . work.' She made me promise to join her on the 25th, so I will be unable to be with you." Each message was personally signed: "Yours, Thomas A. Edison."

The 1950 UX agenda included the communications function, but not in the usual fashion. It listed Smith as a featured speaker on the first day, with the topic "Successful Business-Building Techniques." He analyzed in great detail the actual views of different people throughout a typical U.S. town – his old favorite, Horseheads, NY – and then showed how MPA actions translated directly into sales and market development.

The word "advertising" showed up only once in his talk. Instead, he explored and exploited the essence of marketing and sales in the conduct of business. More than anything else, Smith demonstrated to the executives present that A&SP was an integral part of GE's business and exerted far more than a cosmetic effect on its success.

"Goodnight, Chet." "Goodnight, David"

UX conferences were the most successful spin-off from the More Power to America program, and A&SP marshalled massive resources for follow-ons. In 1954, again at the Island, the theme was "The Electrical Industry in 1964," and A&SP signed up the network news team of Chet Huntley and David Brinkley to set the stage. Four years later, at Woodside, California, atomic power dominated the agenda.

Later conferences at sites like Lake Placid and Williamsburg traded heavily on such current topics as computers and electronics. The bonds between GE and utility executives, however, became more tenuous following the anti-trust cases of 1959, and even more so because of massive turnover in managements, reinforced by a widespread trend away from technical interests to those of the legal and financial world.

GE made a last stab at revitalizing UX in 1973 at the Homestead. The company unveiled plans for a sort of junior grade MPA called "The Second Electrical Century." The focus, however, was heavily on advertising and sales promotion, to be funded mainly by GE, and it never caught fire in the pocketbook. A&SP made some half-hearted moves to launch a series of mini-UX conferences as part of the Second Electrical Century program, dubbed C-II, but the UX concept sputtered and died out.

Flight plan for 747s

A&SP knew that the fuel needed to rekindle the warmth of customers would best come from the excitement of another kind of MPA train. So, logically, A&SP proposed a latter-day version: three Boeing 747s crammed full of GE technology, including not only a diverse group of products but the GE engines and avionics that made the monsters go.

The proposal flickered feebly a couple of times, once when GE geared up to go after the automation market in the '70s, and again in the '80s as a way to dramatize the company's Marketing Renaissance. A&SP also proposed building a spanking new commercial/residential/industrial complex that would be a showcase city for virtually every product and service offered by GE. But the department could never entice a top executive to become angel for the production.

Other conferences, however, kept A&SP writers and producers on the move. Usually, they focused on industries or large customer groups – automation, for example, electronics, the iron and steel industry, appliance dealers, whatever.

At times, AVCOM presented the total offerings of GE to top executives of *Fortune* 500 companies. Where the stakes were extraordinarily high, AVCOM might produce a motion picture for one person, as it did for the CEO of a major steel company.

As a leave-behind, A&SP re-packaged the story in an elaborate brochure, with a cover made of the high-quality sheet metal the proposed new GE equipment would turn out.

Often, a large portion of AVCOM output remained inside the company, particularly during the Reg Jones era when strategic plans of all basic GE business units were reviewed regularly by the corporate executive office. These were crucial to the fortunes of component managers, so they all tried to one-up the presentations of peers as to number of colors, projectors, pages, flashing formats . . . the works.

Welch and "Show 'n Tell"

When Jack Welch took over, he cut out regular reviews. He recognized that GE planning had reached an advanced stage of Show 'n Tell and, furthermore, that he had been part of the process on his road up. So he passed the word that henceforth, presentations to the executive office would be restricted to black and white on a single overhead projector. This put everybody on an equal basis so no one seemed to mind, except the folks in AVCOM who saw a huge chunk of their business vanish overnight.

An A&SP assignment in AVCOM was considered a plum for several reasons. It was unique, first, in that it erased the usual A&SP account boundaries. The world of the AVCOM producer was the considerable world of General Electric.

It was not unusual to switch from a presentation for a smokestack industry one day to the hype of hi-tech the next. Or to draft a speech in the executive offices at Fairfield, followed the day after by one for a sales manager in Coshocton. Or to do scripting, as in the '60s, for the A&SP-produced Distribution Products Road Show, with music scored by Ebb and Kantor, who shortly thereafter did their own thing in "Cabaret." Or, to rub shoulders at the '73 UX conference with a young musician named Barry Manilow who said he deserved a break with MacDonalds because of the jingle he was trying to sell them.

Policy on demand

AVCOM also lent a sense of power to the speechwriter. At times, this was more real than imagined. Some of it stemmed from GE's early forays into market development while staking a claim to leadership.

Over the years, for example, GE executives fondly recalled that Chet Lang had been a a "daring prophet" when he projected during the 1950 UX conference that the demand for electricity in the U.S. would reach one trillion kilowatt-hours by 1970. This was not exactly the product of regimented GE market research.

Ed O'Hora and I, both assigned to do speeches for the conference, sat around one day dreaming up ideas that Ed could put in Lang's speech. I reminded him the experts had warned it would be an unlikely stretch for the country to hit even 900 billion kilowatt-hours. "I know," he said. "But a trillion has a nice ring to it. I think I'll use it anyway."

He did, and that was the market development goal that the industry slavishly adhered to for the next two decades.

The mantle of power passed to AVCOM speechwriters could be a mixed blessing. It wasn't all that unusual when the vice president and general manager of the Apparatus Sales Division called me in during the early '50s, told me the title of a speech assigned to him for a conference and said "You tell me what to say."

Being new to the task and naive, I did, and he bought it. But not the conference committee, which recognized the draft did not follow the formula for a sound speech: tell them what you're going to tell them; tell them; then tell them what you told them. The speech did not tell the audience right off the objective of the message, as shown so well in this example provided by Joan A'Hearn, when she was with AVCOM: "I propose to discuss socialism for the next hour or so, and I'll begin with my conclusion: I'm against it."

So it was back to basic Go, this time to lay more carefully the policy planks a writer needs to build a solid speech.

Some GE people had a special knack for speechwriting at the highest executive levels. Corporate Public Relations' John Garrison offered A&SPers a peek from a seminar in 1973: ". . . This is a somewhat special kind of communications. Moreover, in terms of speech writing, this is where it's at . . . what enables mere English majors to get their hands on some bread. Writing for the chief executive . . . is a profession in which there is no continuity of service. Thus, Ken Patrick wrote for Charlie Wilson, Bob Fegley (of A&SP) wrote for Cordiner, I wrote for Fred Borch. Now Bob has been re-cycled to write for Reg Jones – which is practically equivalent to the 'Second Coming.' At any rate, I know no precedent for it in political or corporate speech writing."

Jack Welch's speechwriter: Jack Welch

Jack Welch broke the mold. He will lean on a speech writer in Corporate Public Relations to organize issues out of a world of facts and layer on logic. But as with any of his meetings, the action starts when he walks in the room; his speeches are mostly his own. After the fact and on paper, the words don't reflect all of the fire and verve. But in person, he's forceful and relates emotionally to the viewer. The same is true on television, to the benefit of both.

Down in the AVCOM engine room, a yawning gap often opened up between writer and speaker that was impossible to bridge. One occurred, typically, during the preparation of a UX conference speech I was doing for the vice president and general manager of GE's Transmission Products Division.

His topic was not exactly spine-tingling – reliability. So to liven things up, I proposed to have a tightrope walker balance his way over the audience while to the rear a gigantic screen would magnify the awesome sights and sounds of Niagara. After 14 drafts and a command reversion to drawings instead of the daredevil, I gave up and let the speaker plod on to ordained boredom.

Informally, AVCOM kept track of such speech re-drafts, to see who claimed the record. As far as we could tell, this was the winner.

In spite of such detractions, AVCOM became a magnet for interesting things and interesting people.

In the early days of A&SP, motion pictures were the lodestone. Edison recognized their potential, commissioning in 1909 what is considered the first industrial-sponsored film, on appliances, entitled "Every Husband's Opportunity." Ten years later, a young GE engineer named Charles A. Hoxie developed the first of a series of patented devices which led to sound-on-film motion pictures. As a result, GE produced sound movies more than a year before America's first talking picture, "The Jazz Singer," with Al Jolson.

Coming attractions: Bette Davis, Dick Powell, etc.

The list of performers in GE commercial films reads like the coming attractions for an Academy Awards reunion: Bette Davis, Dick Powell (with promotion tied to his commercial hit "42nd Street"), Bruce Cabot (he wooed Faye Wray in the original "King Kong"), Mike Nichols and Elaine May, etc.

AVCOM also proved an ideal place for newcomers to flex their cinematic wings. I had been with A&SP less than two years, for example, when Stan Smith asked me to look into a movie on GE's development of the first jet engine in the U.S.

I'd never done a movie before, but with the encouragement of Ray Bonta, who later headed AVCOM, I prepared a seven page treatment outline. Stan bought off on it and a month later, we signed a contract with a Hollywood producer and "The Jet Story" was on its way. It became one of the popular and widely shown films made by GE.

About the same time, another newcomer – Doug Benton, a graduate of the University of New Mexico – crashed and burned doing audio visual acrobatics at GE. This didn't put much of a dent in Doug's career, because he went on to become a highly successful Hollywood producer.

Doug had made various movies with A&SP but his real love was TV. Since Corporate Advertising was where most of that GE action was, he left A&SP to join up. Soon thereafter, Stan Smith arrived to take over as vice president of Marketing and Public Relations in New York City. Stan was Doug's boss again, although a few steps removed. Doug's immediate manager was Dave Burke, the head of Corporate Advertising, who earlier had headed AVCOM in A&SP.

Doug was on his own in New York during a three month span when Dave attended GE's Crotonville Management Institute. So Doug decided to experiment with a TV Christmas spot that had no dialogue. As Dave noted later, it was "a sort of 'cinéma vérité' message, with the story reflected in the faces of children." To appreciate how revolutionary this was for GE, keep in mind that the company had only recently cut loose from its long-time TV sponsorship of Fred Waring and his semi-classical orchestra, the Royal Pennsylvanians.

When Smith returned and with no advance warning saw the spot aired, he ordered Dave to fire Doug. Which Dave did. Actually, he lined up a job for Doug in Hollywood with the executive producer of the GE Theatre. With that entrée, Doug went on to produce such successful series as Boris Karlov's "Thriller," "Dr. Kildare," "The Man From U.N.C.L.E.," "Policewoman" with Angie Dickinson, and other network productions.

At the time when Dave and Doug were with A&SP in Schenectady, another AVCOM writer also did some fancy film work, creating a stir of a different kind. Jack Drummey, fresh from Holy

Cross, and new to AVCOM, landed a spare-time assignment: prepare a skit for the A&SP Christmas party.

Xmas excesses

A&SP Christmas parties were not your ordinary booze and bounce affairs. These were lavish productions, planned months in advance, with a full array of acts, sketches, music and whatever, all staged before a formal dinner and dancing. With uncanny luck, the entertainment invariably honed in on AVCOM.

Jack decided to do a movie. But not just an ordinary one. He wrote and produced a Keystone Cops classic, costuming trainees as chasers and the chased. In a long, low open touring car, the cops caromed back and forth up the broad expanse of Erie Boulevard, then shook their nightsticks as they waited in line while their quarry stopped for a snort at Nicholaus' bar, for a visit with Santa in Barney's department store, for check-in at the main gate of the GE plant, and again in the home corridors of Building 6.

No one bothered to tote up the costs since it came from in-house talent. In fact, it would have caused no more concern than any normal A&SP job. If it were a smash, no one ever questioned the cost. And Drummey's movie was the hit of the evening.

In the '60s, Gerry Sheahan wrote a parody on prize awards at A&SP Christmas parties which was uncomfortably close to the truth: "Drafting has won the display competition with an effort that incorporates 3 selsyns, a shunt wound motor, 3 rectifiers, 18 pounds of styrofoam, 30 pounds of Textolite and two dwarfs which they've hired for the occasion. General reaction is that it is in poor taste but reputed cost of $4,700 outweighs this consideration."

The Rickover incident

An AVCOM assignment brought front seat viewing of a fascinating parade of people, both inside and outside the company. One might be on assignment, for example, when Admiral Rickover came to town to see how GE was doing with the nuclear propulsion facility it operated for the U.S. Navy. On one visit, he inspected a nearby base the day before GE and Niagara Mohawk were, for the first time, to feed nuclear-generated electricity into a commercial power system from a prototype submarine reactor.

There was much last minute work to be done, and everyone knew there was only one way to do it – Rickover's. Well, almost every one.

According to the story, which may be apochryphal, the Admiral was incensed to see what he thought to be a sailor slouched against a building, faded blue fatigues awry, coffee cup in hand. Rickover strode sharply up to the gob, swatted his coffee cup to the ground, and barked: "What outfit are you with sailor?"

The man, who loomed large over Rickover, stared as if eyeing a fly. He then straightened up to his full height, grabbed the frail Admiral by the collar, suspended him close to his face with one hand, and snarled: "I'm with the AFL-CIO, and who the bleep do you think you are?"

As the 1950s began to pick up steam, AVCOM saw an ever broadening circle of GE people call for help in promoting products and careers. From next door in Building 2, GE headquarters in the Schenectady Works, came Russ McFall, who shortly would leave the company to become head of Western Union. Al Cartwright leaned on AVCOM as he began his steady rise to CEO of Canadian General Electric. As did Phil Klass who later flew to McGraw-Hill to become the respected senior avionics editor of *Aviation Week*.

AVCOM handled speeches for others who were soon to become known throughout GE – a marketer named Fred Borch in the Lamp Divison in Cleveland, and a couple of self-styled "bean counters" in Schenectady and Philadelphia, Gerald Phillippe and Reginald Jones.

GE recruiters did not yet have a bead on another enterprising young man named Jack Welch. In a few months, he would leave high school in Boston to explore options in engineering at the University of Massachusetts.

A&SP, meanwhile, reached a pinnacle of influence within the GE hierarchy.

The movers and doers within GE looked to it as their preferred agency of record. They called on A&SP, and most often AVCOM, to take on the big and the spectacular. This was largely due to Stan Smith, who not only breathed first life into AVCOM but shaped the function to his vision of leadership.

With AVCOM, A&SP carried out far more functions than that expected of an outside agency. A&SP also differed from them in that it was part of a very large, highly centralized GE client organization. Its parent, Apparatus Sales, conducted all marketing to outside customers, in effect "buying" goods from the GE manufacturing plants and pricing as it saw fit.

Therefore, as an integral part of this activity, A&SP not only served as the agency but, thanks to the forceful role of Smith in this power center, also controlled the ad budgets.

This was, to say the least, at odds with the normal role of an advertising agency. But that was about to change.

IV

BREAKING UP

The ad manager of the newly formed GE product department turned over rough layout, copy and artwork for an ad to A&SP account supervisor Tommy Allen. The latter asked for the objective so A&SP could offer an alternative. To which his client said: "My objective is to run this picture and this copy in this magazine." Then, with fire in his eye, he told Tommy: "If you're interested in my business from now on, you won't change a word."

By 1952, there was a hint of change in the air at GE. It was hard to tell if it would coalesce into a storm cloud or a glowing opportunity for A&SP.

The change was decentralization. Ralph Cordiner, named president to replace the retiring Charlie Wilson, was determined to more closely manage the mushrooming growth of the company, which over the past 20 years had gone from $147 million to nearly $3 billion in sales. The dignified, scholarly new chief executive chose a textbook approach to the challenge: he commissioned textbooks to spell out his solution.

Smiddy and the Blue Books

These were the famous GE Blue Books, a five-volume edition which, according to the American Management Association, set forth "the first well-documented philosophy for any corporate structure." The author's name became familiar to all white collar employees: Harold Smiddy. Every GE manager poured over the more than 1,000 pages which spelled out in infinite detail the four key Cordiner dictums: plan; organize; integrate; measure.

All of this was to take place in 83 new product departments, each to be run like a separate business with its own general manager. For the first time, too, the advertising function was moved out from under sales and given equal billing. Both – along with product planning, market research, product service, marketing personnel, and marketing administration – were grouped under the new umbrella of marketing. Marketing, in turn, was propped up on a level with the old standbys of engineering, manufacturing, finance, legal, and employee relations.

The potential storm cloud for A&SP was etched sharply in the charter of the marketing managers. Since they along with the other managers now had profit and loss responsibility, they also were given freedom to choose whatever resources they needed to achieve it. Translation: they could go to an outside advertising agency to handle their work if they wanted to. A&SP would have to prove its worth.

Some of the younger, more enlightened A&SP managers saw this as opportunity. It was their chance, for the first time, to move into the arena of real agencies, and to compete like one.

Decentralization: culture shock

For old timers, however, it was culture shock of the first magnitude. It brought with it all the awful aspects of adolescence. You knew that if you wanted to go to the Prom, you had to ask someone for a date. But you didn't quite know how to go about it since you'd never been in this fix before. Plus, just thinking about that first knock on the door made you wobbly all over.

Stan Smith dissolved the dilemma in his usual pragmatic style. He ignored it. Stan marshalled a platoon of new account supervisors who could double in copy and contact, and sent us off to knock on doors and, if need be, break them down. His strategy was simple: smother the marketing and ad managers like a blanket and leave them with the impression that A&SP was their only source and their only choice.

Actually, A&SP was better geared to the agency environment than one might expect, in spite of its previous monastic mode. From the early days of the company, GE people had kept in close touch with the U.S. advertising community.

A GE advertising man named Frank Davis co-founded ABC, the Audit Bureau of Circulation. In 1918, he also conducted what was probably the first GE market and advertising research study, certainly one of the earliest for the industry, with field work by Eastman Research.

Bruce Barton and GE

GE also consorted with a succession of agencies, beginning with Batten Barton Durstine and Osborn in 1923 for a corporate campaign. BBDO's chief copywriter, Bruce Barton – and a founder just three years earlier – was the only non-GE member on the company's first advertising council.

Other early agencies retained by GE's centralized advertising function included Lord & Thomas and Logan, which later became Foote, Cone and Belding, and the Maxon Agency in 1936 for a brand new ad program on R&D. A&SP also selected the G. M. Basford Co. of New York to give advice and counsel and to prep some ads when A&SP began positioning itself in 1952 to serve decentralized company components.

For its new role, however, A&SP had more going for it than mere association with the industry and outside agencies.

From the turn of the century when it was a part of something called the Supply Department, the forerunner of A&SP pioneered classic ad strategies and techniques along with such early advertising greats as Claude C. Hopkins and Earnest Elmo Calkins. In fact, for the first quarter century *all* GE ads were produced in-house.

Ad pioneering

GE introduced color into its advertising in 1901. Whereas Hopkins concluded that "no test that I know of proves such expense profitable," GE decided that color used functionally could prove to retailers that incandescent light displayed merchandise far more realistically than arc lamps.

GE had also run editorial ads as early as 1905, followed shortly thereafter by ones which featured before-and-after comparisons, sweepstakes, seasonal selling, crime and accident prevention, and – while it's hard to believe in the context of today's staid company – even a racy, female nude.

GE's first corporate ad appeared in 1916, including a stab at a standard format. GE people then showed traits of later A&SP types – they mustered all their creative powers to circumvent anything standard. The format soon became fuzzy and disappeared. Only the GE monogram, introduced in 1910 and affectionately known thereafter as The Meatball, survived.

And so, armed perhaps as much with tradition as with practical experience, the troops of A&SP marched forth for the first time to seek contact on unfamiliar ground with their newly appointed counterparts in the decentralized components. The reception, not to mention the road, earned mixed reviews.

The natives were friendly in Pittsfield, Massachusetts, the centralized spawning ground for various transformer and capacitor lines that were later cast adrift as separate departments in New York, North Carolina, Georgia, and Florida. The deportment in Pittsfield was due, most likely, to the genteel outlook one found in old-line GE businesses. It was in this case a factory founded in 1890 by William Stanley and taken over by GE shortly after the turn of the century.

Riding the GE "Canonball"

The A&SP account team reveled even more in the transportation to and from Pittsfield. A long, black Cadillac limousine called the "GE Cannonball" ferried visitors from portal to portal, with all the grace and comfort that top executives enjoy today.

Travelling to most other GE locations from Schenectady was something else, generally by train and generally an ordeal. A&SPers calling on the GE motor plant in Ft. Wayne, Indiana, for example, were also whisked to the plant by company car. Unfortunately, the train dumped passengers at a remote town called Waterloo on the outskirts of Ft. Wayne at 5 a.m., while the GE transportation didn't show until two and one half hours later.

A&SP teams going by train to the GE plant in Lynn, just outside Boston, faced a dreary, overnight run through the Berkshires, including the Hoosac Tunnel. There was some consolation – on one trip, the train actually ran out of fuel, which one could tolerate more easily than if it had happened today in an airplane.

Lynn was also fertile ground for GE growth businesses, many of which prospered elsewhere on their own – outdoor lighting, which moved to North Carolina; rectifiers, which later blossomed in various locations as GE's semiconductor business; jet engines, a spin-off from land-based turbines long located in Lynn as well as Schenectady; meters, which in the early '50s skittered up the coast to New Hampshire; and GE instruments, which stayed put until sold in the '70s to a Japanese firm.

And then there was Erie

And then there was Erie. Erie which, on the northwestern tip of

Pennsylvania, gets "lake effect" weather from the great lake for which it is named. Erie, which gets rained on an average of 163 days each year. Erie, which more than once has had close to five feet of snow in December alone.

"Erie isn't the end of the world," the former GE transportation ad manager, Steve Adams, said in 1984. Then, with a half smile, he added: "But you can see it from here."

Dreary Erie, the Mistake by the Lake.

This is probably unfair. But to put it in perspective, you would have to take the overnight sleeper from Schenectady to Erie every other week for two years, as I did as an A&SP account supervisor, then judge for yourself.

The reception in Erie was cordial, but cool. Stan Smith wanted to apply his "Pat and Goose" method to the railroads through a new advertising campaign in *U.S. News & World Report, Time* and *Newsweek.* "Take this campaign out there," he boomed, "and don't ask them if they like it. Tell them this is what it's going to be."

He neglected to say what they would certainly conclude: they'd have to pay for it, too.

If the approach had been made six months later, an A&SP account rep very likely would have been sent packing, but I was not. Grudgingly, Erie accepted the proposal. The spirit of independence brewing among product department clients had not fermented enough for them to make a clean break with the past.

Even so, the whiffs of freedom created a heady vision. A&SP clients soon would no longer be lackeys, no longer dictated to. It was now *their* turn to have their say. And uppermost in their minds was the chance to tout their own products. After all, that was what they were measured on. Let somebody else worry about the rest of the company, and let somebody else worry about the company as a whole. They could now do their own thing, like real marketing, sales and ad managers were supposed to.

This attitude was further complicated because some product departments had become dumping grounds for A&SP castoffs. This posed continual problems in account handling. A&SP tried to promote camaraderie and GE unity of purpose through occasional joint meetings with clients, but they weren't very effective.

To forestall the temptation to defect, Smith devised a twofold strategy: first, prepare superior work that moved boldly beyond what anybody on the outside was doing, and second, build from a solid communications platform that would counteract splintering and present the company at its synergistic best. Again, no outside agency could realistically do this.

Smith's "Creative Effective Advocate"

Any A&SPer could rise to the challenge if he or she became a "Creative Effective Advocate." The words were vintage Smith.

Don't be "cowed" by technical matters, he began. And never, ever "fudge the evidence" or "kowtow" to rank. Marshall whatever forces you need – "blasting, managing, etc. as may be required." Cultivate a "high frustration tolerance." Be willing to indulge in an "intolerable labor of thoughts."

A torrent of words spilled over the two pages: integrity, courage, intuition, simplicity, ethical standards, ability, perspective, respect, style – all energized by such verbs as grasp, understand, appeal, reinforce, illuminate, withstand, synthesize.

Stan's clincher: "An outstanding creative effective advocate will provide leadership in synthesizing different viewpoints, readily accepting better ideas, rejecting inferior ones, and slaughtering his own brain children as required."

It's a shame Smith didn't cross paths with William Faulkner during the latter's brief foray into advertising. Faulkner once expressed a kindred credo, when interviewed for the *Paris Review* in 1956: "The writer's only responsibility is to his art. He will be completely ruthless if he is a good one. He has a dream. It anguishes him so much he must get rid of it. He has no peace until then. Everything goes by the boards: honor, pride, decency, security, happiness, all, to get the book written. If a writer has to rob his mother, he will not hesitate: the 'Ode on a Grecian Urn' is worth any number of old ladies."

A&SP did produce some outstanding creative work during that period. It's difficult to say if this was due to Smith's dictum or because he assembled a mix of good people and then gave them the freedom to do their own thing. It's also debatable whether it could not have been done by anybody on the outside. During this period some of his best people defected to do the same sort of work elsewhere.

Trout and Ries: roots

One of them, Al Ries, left to form and head a New York City agency, Ries Cappiello Colwell. This would later change to Trout and Ries, bolstered by another ex-A&SPer, Jack Trout.

Encouraged by the benevolent reception in Pittsfield, Ries

while with GE created and launched a program called ATANA (All Transformers Are Not Alike) which is still remembered by people who were in that business. As late as 1979, A&SPer Bob Ingmire called it "one of the all-time greatest of GE advertising programs," because it integrated ads, promotion, PR, and packaged audio visual programs in a way that won a five per cent market share from four competitors in just 18 months.

ATANA was an early example of positioning. While various other A&SPers staked a claim to this during their stay with GE, both Ries and Trout built their careers on it. In 1985, they stretched a string of speeches, articles and seminars on the subject into a book called "Positioning: The Battle for Your Mind." The publisher, McGraw-Hill, has since released two more by the authors: "Marketing Warfare" and, new in 1989, "Bottom-up Marketing," which tells how to turn tactics into coherent strategy.

Another A&SPer decided that his "thing" was to emulate the early GE ad with the nude. Actually, he did it tastefully, and the result was functionally effective. He prepared a full page bleed photo of a belly dancer entwined in a new GE power cable, with the one-word headline: "Flexible." While this might be acceptable today, it was at odds with the austere Cordiner image, and never made it beyond proof.

Peddling a locomotive via direct response

Smith liked experimentation, so I decided to try some direct response advertising. This was everyday fodder at my former agency, Bozell & Jacobs, in Omaha, Nebraska – I'd used it often marketing seed corn, hog and poultry medicine, and other things agricultural.

The four-page, black and white direct response ad for GE documented the substantial savings an industrialist could expect by swapping an old steam locomotive for a newly developed GE diesel-electric to do in-plant switching.

A few days after the ad ran, I got a call from the president of a small industrial firm in eastern Pennsylvania. He had contacted the A&SP Distribution Center through the number keyed to the coupon on the back page. "I saw your ad on locomotives," he said. "I want to buy one."

So I referred him to the nearest GE salesman and he did buy a locomotive, for $200,000. Unfortunately, we couldn't brag about it because the customer wasn't "indexed" – he hadn't been identified by the sales force as a prospect, and it would have been embarrassing to GE field sales if we had publicized it.

While there was freedom on the part of every A&SPer to sharpen skills on product promotion, Stan Smith constantly stressed the need to promote the company as a whole. The UX conference, begun with the MPA program, was a notable example.

Stan also initiated a series of so-called Industry Advertising programs. Products and components were grouped by market interest in industry books – the "Designers Digest," for example, was keyed to the interest of electronics engineers.

Even individual market advertising was aligned to the effort. One ad featured a complicated cutaway drawing of Grand Central Station, showing a host of GE products throughout underground levels – locomotives, transit cars, power cable, transformers, switchgear, air conditioning, lighting, and so on.

Stan recognized the potential of consumer periodicals in promoting industrial goods. He initiated a series of multi-page ads in magazines such as the *Saturday Evening Post, LOOK* and *LIFE.* A typical subject was aircraft engines, ostensibly for the nation's defense, but the copy quickly noted they derived from long term GE work in ground-based turbines for utilities, railroads, and industrial businesses.

A&SP also gained great mileage in consumer books through merchandising. A product ad would be inserted in a single regional or city edition of a publication, at low cost, and then broadly distributed through direct mail with a covering letter and a banner on the ad that shouted: "As advertised in *TIME!*" or whatever. Low postage rates then in effect made wide-scale mailings economically attractive.

Positioning GE

There was really never any argument about who started positioning in A&SP. Smith was a master at it. Any happening was the occasion for him to rise.

One came on GE's 75th anniversary. This was not exactly a breathtaking moment in anybody's view, but he decided to make it one.

Stan was a firm believer in the Better Mousetrap theory. In fact, this became the theme of many of his talks on the virtues of promoting product innovations. So, on the occasion of the company's 75th birthday, he again fanned out the troops to identify GE product "firsts" in every area of the company. The number was predetermined at 63, because he envisioned 16 pages, covering four "firsts" per page, with one box reserved for the sign-off.

The ad presentation *was* impressive, with firsts ranging from appliance motors to aircraft armament controls, from sawmill drives to lamp ballasts. It was a bit of a stretch for some – who remembers the first "cast in concrete reactor"? Or even what it was for? But the insert made up the largest single ad placed in business magazines up to that time. In *Business Week,* 98% of those who read the issue (86% of total subscribers) also read the ad, which appeared in January 1953.

Individual contributor vs. manager

Along with this continuing strong dose of leadership, Smith doled out the Cordiner Blue Books. That measured approach to management was almost antithetical to Stan's style, so the books didn't cause much of a stir. Except one. That was the add-on volume for "The Role of the Individual Contributor," prepared to assuage the sensibilities of those who wanted to just do their own work within GE and not manage people.

The concept was anathema to A&SP trainees. Not be a manager? As anyone who ever went through the training program well knew, that was the name of the game in A&SP. And the first step was to become an ACCOUNT SUPERVISOR!

The title at A&SP didn't carry the clout it does on Madison Avenue; it was really the equivalent of an account executive. But it was the first step up the management ladder so clearly defined in the initial four Blue Books and, therefore, it meant almost everything.

Possibly the only thing that mattered more than a manager's title, particularly if you asked on a rainy or snowy day in Schenectady, was an S plate. This was a little metal tag that bolted on the front bumper of your car so you could drive past the guards at the gate and park inside the plant.

In 1952, there were 40,750 employees at the Schenectady plant, half the number of people in the city. Without the magic parking permit, one who forgot to note where he parked could commonly spend a half hour thrashing through a sea of cars.

The aura of the S-Plate is epitomized in the office of Chuck Hanley, who along with George Schubert left A&SP in 1973 and shortly formed their own audio visual firm, Light & Power Productions in Scotia, New York, later selling it to employees in a leveraged buy-out. Both Chuck and George maintain strong ties to the A&SP and GE community, but only one evidence of the bond is displayed in Chuck's office – a desk ornament made up of a plastic-encased S Plate.

In the spirit of the Blue Books, A&SPers did their best to breathe life into the Cordiner precepts. One of them – goal setting – was the key to successful planning and measurement, but it posed problems with product departments.

Planning fever

Russ Bowersox, the ad manager for urban transit in Erie, became thoroughly exasperated with A&SP's insistence on planning. "My objective with this ad," he once said, in all seriousness, "is to run it in the association's convention issue so they'll give me a good seat at the sessions. Last year I had to sit behind a post."

Another ad manager, John McLaughlin of the Instrument Department in Lynn, totally caught the planning fever incubating in the Blue Books. In fact, he bordered on the delirious when he showed up as guest at an A&SP Planning Board, and plopped on the conference table a three-foot long library of plans books for his single product line. No one had seen anything like it before nor, gratefully, did they afterwards.

Planning sprouted everywhere. The general manager of GE's Service Shops Department in Schenectady, Howard McCullough, wasn't much at committing plans to paper, but at each annual business review, with a straight face he would allow as how this year, he was budgeting for one, two or whatever number of hurricanes. These represented business volume he expected to gain from cleaning up after each mess.

In a way, this period of the company's development seemed to A&SP a kind of twilight zone. It was almost the reverse of adolescence – a strange mixture of the old giving way to the new.

First radio, first TV

On their rounds of the company, A&SPers rubbed shoulders with living legends. On the main avenue of the Schenectady Works, one often saw but was seldom seen by the absent-minded Ernst Alexanderson. The Swedish-born GE inventor built an alternator for the world's first radio broadcast, was the first to transmit a facsimile message across the Atlantic, and staged the first home reception of television.

Later, one watched television in Schenectady on WRGB, the GE station which in 1939 gained the first U.S. license. The call letters came from the station's namesake, W. R. G. Baker. As vice president of GE's television receiver business, Baker ignored the advice of his marketing research experts who said customers wanted ever larger consoles. Baker heeded his own intuition: he introduced small, inexpensive portables, stimulated demand through saturation advertising, and enlarged the market enormously.

At the corporate R&D Lab on the outskirts of town, one could sense as well as see the dignified presence of Dr. William Coolidge, inventor of the X-Ray tube, and Dr. Irving Langmuir, GE's first Nobel Prize winner. One would not have seen the lab's director, Dr. Willis Whitney, one noontime when he retired behind his own office door, literally wrapped up in his work – on the floor, with outer clothing removed, testing the controls of a newly developed GE product, the electric blanket.

It would be rare to find someone like him today, bouncing from lab to lab with the query: "Are you having fun?" And how refreshing it would be to have someone reaffirm his outlook on science: "The vision is dazzling in its beauty and its vast reaches. This world is truly the Garden of the Gods. But we have not even begun to taste its fruits. As yet we are eating grass."

Many GE engineers, God bless them, lived in a world of their own. Each foray into their thought process was an adventure.

Listen to this one analyzing Carl Ally's nemesis, the GE Schenectady Works cafeteria: "The average time required by a customer, from the pay-as-you-enter cash desk until he is served and seated is less than a minute . . . Adjacent to the nearer end of the belt conveyor the ticket is exchanged for an aluminum tray . . . these belts travel at the rate of 65 feet per minute and allow 15 seconds for the customer to select his food."

And savor the sweet naiveté of this one, quoted from a book published by A&SP in 1919 when it was called the Publication Bureau, with an introduction by E. W. Rice, Jr., GE's president: "Schenectady, a city of 97,000 population, has no 'red light district.' On the contrary, it has plenty of good entertainment which is more available here than in larger cities. For instance, the American Institute of Electrical Engineers has meetings twice a month . . ."

"More like customers than anyone"

While A&SP was sustained by its roots in the past, it flourished largely through the rich diversity of its environment. Consider, for example, that in the early 1950s General Electric was engaged in 13 of the 21 basic U.S. manufacturing industries and sold its products into all 21. As A&SP's Dave Jones later summed up: "We're more like our customers than anyone else."

In Schenectady alone, A&SPers dealt with five GE groups, 11 divisions, four major corporate components, 55 operations at the product department level, and seven laboratories, located in more than 200 buildings in 17 area locations. They also associated daily with a host of sales and service organizations which flooded the business world through every conceivable sales channel – retail, wholesale, distributor, OEM, influence, political, governmental, you name it.

As if that cultivation weren't enough, GE nourished various wholly owned subsidiaries – the East Erie Commercial Railroad, the Mahoning Valley Steel Company, the Chicago Castings Company, the Electric Mutual Liability Insurance Company, the Maqua Printing Company, the GE radio and TV broadcasting company, the GE Credit Corporation, plus others concerned with real estate, distributors, overseas operations, and so on. Not to mention a phone system that, next to AT&T, was the largest private industrial telecommunications network in the world . . . and an A&SP client.

All of this posed an exhilarating challenge for A&SP: how to communicate to this tremendously complex marketplace an equally complex offering of GE goods and services. Just coming to grips with the products alone was mind-boggling.

The mind-boggling world of GE products

Most estimates peg the number of GE products at about 200,000. Yet a 1951 MPA training course noted "It's possible to choose from over 100,000 different GE motors, considering all mechanical and operational features." Another GE product line – lamps – boasted that it made 10,000 different types of lamp bulbs. So the real GE total is probably beyond a quarter of a million products.

For the record, nobody ever toted up the number of GE products produced, but the total would be staggering. In 1985, the annual report said GE turned out 29 million motors alone.

Of course, GE makes all kinds of appliances and electronic equipment. And most businessmen are familiar with such things as GE transformers and switchgear, aircraft jet engines, propulsion turbines for the Navy, magnetic resonance systems for hospitals, ICs, radar, and engineered materials. The list seems endless.

If you were buying GE electrical equipment to make a coal mine more productive, the company offered roof bolts to keep the shafts from caving in. If you were running a GE diesel-electric locomotive, you'd find in the Apparatus Handbook a listing for a replacement toilet.

Out at the R&D Lab, you could watch an experimental GE vehicle as big as an elephant lumbering over rough terrain on four legs, or hook a ride in a sleek, battery-powered electric car. You might smile to see technicians use baby diapers to clean the tops as well as bottoms of a newly discovered, clear plastic called Lexan. You might muse with Ralph Alpher on how he noodled out the Big Bang theory on the creation of the universe. And you could ask the scientists if they'd yet proved the thesis that you can make diamonds out of peanut butter.

Even the unflappable Jack Trout, as an A&SP trainee, was taken aback at the challenge of one GE product. The client, tucked away in the loft of an ancient factory in the Schenectady Works, sintered messy black powder into carbon brushes for electric motors. After a sales call, Jack came back with a half dazed look to report: "They make dirt!"

Expert back-up

Fortunately, A&SPers had plenty of help in bringing all of these factors into focus. For every problem, a simple search uncovered an uncommon expert.

Somewhere in GE, there lurked a near perfect profile of every conceivable business influence. In Engineering Services, for example, the expertise gained by all manufacturing managers throughout the company was daily distilled in Schenectady by a man named Hank Heddescheimer. In short order, he could put you and your program on track with his counterparts in the world outside of GE.

The same held true for other work functions, sometimes to a ludicrous degree. Once while setting the strategy for an Instrument Department promotion in Lynn, we were told that GE devices had no advantage over competition. "They're all the same," shrugged the GE product specialist.

He did admit, after some probing, that the GE dials were slightly more readable due to the luminosity of the paint used by GE. We then queried the GE engineer who had devoted his entire career to this narrow specialty. His counsel formed the basis for a highly successful campaign on the theme "The Big Look."

Maybe one reason for all this was that for many years GE made an outstanding line of paint under the Glyptal trademark, derived from work on insulating varnishes. Both interior and exterior paints were sold at bargain prices in employee stores until the business was sold in 1985.

The most fertile training ground

Anyone in A&SP in the early 1950s could relate to Whitney's "Garden of the Gods." It was harvest time. The newly decentralized components were flowering with products, the markets were hungry, and both begged to be nurtured with campaigns.

A&SP offered the aspiring young marketer, in the view of many, the most fertile training ground in the world. And it offered something the average industrial client on the outside could not match: a hearing for ideas which, if accepted at the right level of management, would be backed by the considerable resources of the General Electric Company, to the degree needed for success.

How valuable this asset was would soon become apparent.

V

MOTHER LODE

❧

In 1955, an itinerant music peddler approached A&SP with a novel idea: why not launch GE's new "Live Better . . . Electrically" program with a pre-Broadway TV showing of his proposed musical? "Too dicey," we said. So he sought another angel. The composer: Meredith Willson. The show: one of the Great White Way's all-time blockbusters, "The Music Man," starring Robert Preston and Shirley Jones.

By the mid-'50s, the post-World War II boom was clearly fading. Top GE management knew that something had to be done to prop up sales growth.

With sure instincts, General Electric went back to its roots. These were imbedded not so much in products as in electrical usage. Or, in the parlance of utilities, in load.

The "Benign Circle"

The early leaders of GE learned to gauge the effect of electrical load on GE sales through the "benign circle" – the continuous ebb and flow of business through interlocking GE markets. Demand by consumers built business for manufacturers, who in turn called for more power from utilities, who sold to both manufacturers and consumers, and so on. It formed an integral cycle, with electricity the lifeblood. If at any time the flow turned sluggish, GE knew it was time to stir things up.

A business slowdown was the motivation for More Power to America in the mid-'40s. Again in the mid-'50s, it stimulated another case-example market development program, "Live Better . . . Electrically." As usual, A&SP landed in the center of the action.

Market development at its purest: LBE

LBE was the purest form of market development – long-range, industry-wide, targeted to all ages. While it resembled MPA in some respects, there were distinct differences. The most obvious was in consumer demand.

MPA correctly anticipated that with the lifting of wartime controls, there would be a free-flowing surge in consumer spending. The demand would call for all kinds of goods, electrical and otherwise. The primary audience for MPA, then, was the manufacturers who would have to make those goods. And the most efficient process, in GE's view, was electrical.

By 1954, the outlook for consumer demand had reversed. Studies by the company's Marketing Services Division, headed by Vice President Fred Borch, who was to become GE's CEO nine years later, raised serious doubts that the company would reach the optimistic sales goals outlined by President Cordiner for 1965. Again, it all hinged on electrical load. The report forecast a serious softening in one arc of the benign circle – the residential market. If not bolstered, the flow of GE product sales to manufacturers and utilities, which reflected consumer demand, could slow to a trickle.

Target this time: the consumer

LBE, therefore, targeted the consumer as its primary audience, not the manufacturer as with MPA. And since the overriding need was to build load, the primary focus had to be not just *any* goods, but *electrical* goods.

General Electric mulled over the conventional way to launch a market development program: get together with everybody who had a stake in the outcome, solicit time and money and, when you attained a critical mass, go for it.

But the odds for success down this route seemed slim. The number of potential participants was so large that even a steering committee would burst a boardroom.

To begin with, a couple of hundred utilities had the most to gain if LBE were successful – a forecasted doubling of demand for their product, electricity, in slightly more than five years. There were also the appliance manufacturers and dealers and distributors whose prospects were absolutely mind-bending. At that time less than 10 per cent of the nation's wired homes had driers, garbage disposers, or dishwashers. Three and one half million U.S. homes didn't even have refrigerators, while another eight and one half million were without electric clothes washers.

Many homes also had the door slammed shut on the good life because of a wiring bottleneck. Before their residents could add more appliances, or electric heating and air conditioning, they had to upgrade electrical service. That opened up a huge, new potential for architects, contractors, builders and realtors. And, along every step of the way, for the bankers.

Potential investment return: awesome

The answer to the launching dilemma for GE lay in one simple fact: all of these groups were not only potential GE allies, but GE customers. The calculated return from any level of GE investment was awesome and, therefore, irresistible.

So on September 12, 1955, A&SP mailed a formal invitation to the top executives of 144 of the nation's major electric utility companies over Ralph Cordiner's signature. He solicited their participation "to help customers Live Better . . . Electrically," and suggested that "electrical manufacturers can provide the national materials" while "you can spearhead the local activity" with trade allies.

This was really a diplomatic sop to both groups, because GE had already decided that the most efficient way to get the program off the ground, and probably the only one with a reasonable chance for success, was to kick it off alone. GE reasoned that the other logical participants would be pulled in by the sheer weight of GE numbers.

And the numbers committed were substantial: start-up costs of $8 million, plus the considerable clout of tying in all of GE's multi-million dollar consumer advertising. At the same time, the company estimated that the multiplication factor for industry participation would be about 12 to one, adding some $100 million per year to GE's investment. This, GE felt, should build up enough momentum in a few years to turn the program over to an industry group.

All of this was of more than academic interest to A&SP.

In his invitation to utility presidents, Cordiner noted that LBE would be a "long-range *promotional* program." Accordingly, the Plan of Implementation prepared in the President's Office targeted A&SP to do the implementing.

The outline of the "Live Better ... Electrically" program

was relatively simple. The doing, on the other hand, was something else.

Cordiner had listed two objectives for LBE: "Accelerate electrification of American homes and dwellings," and "Improve the nation's standard of living." The single goal: build load. If successful, GE could then sit back and watch the benign circle rev up again.

The complex challenge to A&SP

All that remained for A&SP was to explain and sell the concept to every architect, builder, contractor, lending agency, realtor, electrical manufacturer and distributor and dealer in the country, prepare both national and local materials for each group, and then spell out in infinite detail how to use them.

As if that in itself weren't bad enough, the challenge of marshalling and focusing the efforts of General Electric made the task incredibly complex. Seventy-five GE product departments, each operating very much like a separate business, were tagged to participate in LBE. To coordinate their inputs, initially skewed by short-range skepticism, A&SP formed a 15-member review board.

This board represented almost the entire scope of the company, ranging from both large and small appliances to electronics, apparatus that encompassed motors and switchgear and turbines and transformers, construction materials that swept in component products and lamps, GE Credit and the General Electric Supply Company, plus a small army of field sales divisions. For good measure, A&SP layered in the network of GE commercial vice presidents to take care of high level contacts.

As one of its first moves, A&SP prepared an LBE "Guide for Action" that described for all of these GE people the full scope of the program and their responsibilities.

Strategy: classic push-pull

The strategy for "Live Better . . . Electrically" was two-pronged – classic push-pull. The push by GE was targeted for utilities and the trade allies. The pull was designed to get consumers into their stores and offices.

A&SP anticipated almost every conceivable action in the initial three-phase program planned for utilities.

In phase one, the plan called for each utility to receive in October a 46-page loose leaf program guide outlining the intent, scope and specifics of the different programs, both national and local. The guide would even include a local action "Prospecting" plans book written for a mythical company, General Power and Light. Utilities could copy this literally if they didn't have the time or means to come up with their own.

Phase two centered on a personal presentation prepared by GE for utilities to use in generating interest among trade allies. It would include a brochure outlining a wide-ranging array of tie-in suggestions, as well as samples of material that could be tailored for use with customers. These included direct mail pieces, ad mats and repro art, suggested layouts for point-of-purchase displays, designs for exhibits, truck signs, car cards, billboards and window streamers, mock-ups for newspaper supplements, radio and TV scripts, and so forth.

Courting the consumer

Phase three for utilities encompassed a comprehensive package of LBE consumer promotion for use in the Spring of 1956. A&SP planned a full-color motion picture that could easily be adapted for TV, a 72-page consumer home planning guide, another 64-page booklet on modernizing home wiring, local newspaper advertising, radio and TV scripts, all kinds of tie-in materials like those provided for trade allies, and various programs centered around an Electric Home Contest, Demonstration Home, Demonstration Classes, and on and on.

The other half of the LBE push bracketed the diverse range of trade allies. Theoretically, utilities were to play host to them at kick-off shows around the country in February. But in fact, GE – A&SP, that is – did it all.

The potential audience was so vast and so splintered that A&SP chose a relatively new medium – a nationwide closed circuit television show. This would then be bolstered by a heavy schedule of business and trade advertising, exhibits at key trade shows, and special items for target industries, such as builder specification catalogs, etc.

Then, to capitalize on the traditional Spring selling surge, the other portion of the LBE pincer – the pull – would be launched by GE: a national program aimed at consumers.

Kick-off: nationwide CC-TV

Originally, GE had planned to kick this off with a network TV spectacular, and had listened as Meredith Willson tinkled his way through his proposed show on an old upright piano in an A&SP office. But A&SP decided instead that a blitz of TV spots would be more productive in the light of long-term LBE aims.

The program also included a heavy schedule of two-page spreads in the leading consumer books of the time, such as *LIFE, LOOK* and *The Saturday Evening Post,* plus all the leading women's magazines and shelter books. These were reinforced with another made-for-TV color movie, a national Electric Home contest tied in with local LBE programs and, as a grand prize, an all-electric home loaded with the latest GE residential products. All of this was to be funded by A&SP through LBE.

Two years earlier, in 1953, Stan Smith had moved on to General Public Relations at GE headquarters in New York City. His successor as general manager of A&SP was Ralston B. Reid, a laconic Scotsman with the frame and manner of a Jimmie Stewart.

An initial staff of one

Reid had served almost as an understudy for Smith for some time, and had no hesitation to move forcefully in the mode of Smith. So, with the LBE matrix in place and a go-ahead from the top, Rallie got things rolling with rented space in New York City and a single staffer on temporary duty – me. This was a transitional step to keep things on track during the crucial first nine months.

Shortly thereafter, Reid put in place an LBE project manager, Bob Boian, who hired a staff of 30 to power up the three operational segments: Program Planning, under Phil Hoppin, who had been GE's ad manager for Air Conditioning; Inter-Industry Activities, under Bob Ingmire from A&SP in Schenectady; and Customer Relations, under A&SP's Steve Van Voorhis, who would later become GE's regional vice president in New York City. LBE called upon A&SP in Schenectady for various specialized services – finance and personnel, the news bureau for PR, and the audio-visual section to handle the LBE movies and closed circuit TV show.

The last was a primary order of business because of its complexity. In less than six months, LBE not only had to produce an hour-long extravaganza for simultaneous showing in 76 cities, it had to coordinate the invitations and arrangements for the invited guests to attend local showings hosted by 80 major U.S. utilities. A&SP's Jack O'Connor, now a vice president of Ticketron, drew the lead assignment.

The closed-circuit show represented a bold move then and, more than two decades later, it still stands tall. For example, when IBM introduced its new line of personal computers in

March 1987, characterized by *The Wall Street Journal* as "the most significant . . . since IBM entered the nascent field in summer 1981," it wooed its big corporate customers – "lush sales turf" – with video conference briefings in only 40 cities. Ford Motor Co., introducing the latest versions of its hot-selling Thunderbird and Mercury Cougar in December 1988, beamed entertainer Dick Clark via satellite to 30 locations.

Calling on Show Biz stars

For the LBE show, A&SP signed up two of the premiere TV personalities of that era – John Daly of "What's My Line" and Giselle MacKensie of the "Lucky Strike Hit Parade" – as host and hostess. The project also recruited well-known leaders from electrical, financial, construction and related publishing fields to lend credibility to the program and gain rapport with the audience. The producer commissioned an original score for the show, and auditioned talent from the Broadway stage.

LBE left nothing to chance. Its regional people huddled with every utility to review a 20-page planbook just for the local closed circuit showings. The book deciphered the medium, suggested show locations, proposed a program format, and identified whom to invite. It outlined how to form a program committee (including a detailed program agenda), scoped out sample promotion, mailings, publicity, exhibits, a take-home kit, and follow-up actions. It included a check-list of everything needed for successful staging, rehearsals, printed programs, tickets, even name badges.

The show came off without a hitch. Forty thousand guests attended, the largest audience for any commercial telecast up to that time. To gain additional mileage, LBE prepared a filmed kinescope of the show which utilities then showed to an additional quarter of a million associates and allies in their service areas.

Audience reaction: terrific

Con Ed of New York City, typical of most utilities, reported a "universally favorable reaction." Ohio Power noted "We've needed a cooperative program such as this for many years." Union Electric of St. Louis reported, "audience reaction was terrific"; the Electric League of Los Angeles called it "the finest program we've ever witnessed." Jersey Central liked it "because it's constructive for our company and our people." San Diego Gas and Electric said, "We're behind the program 100%." Gulf Power of Pensacola wrote: "We're getting calls already about plans to tie in with the national campaign." LBE was on its way.

The heavy content of consumer time and space posed a potential problem for A&SP, whose expertise had largely been honed in the industrial marketplace. The solution led to an unusual juxtaposition of talents, whereby one advertising agency, A&SP, hired another advertising agency, BBDO, to handle its account.

This opened up an exciting prospect for A&SP. While BBDO had long handled General Electric's corporate advertising, there had been almost no interchange between BBDO and A&SP. Here, at last, the door opened for A&SP, promising a glimpse into the world of big time advertising agencies. It reflected a glow of kinship, because one of BBDO's founders and its original chief copywriter, Bruce Barton, had been the only outside member of GE's first advertising council established in 1923.

Links with Y&R, BBDO

A&SP had gained an advance peek at the New York agency scene during a visit to Young & Rubicam to solicit LBE tie-ins, through Y&R advertising for GE major appliances. The headquarters reception area and officers' suites of the agency were a far cry from the massive oak and steel furniture of A&SP's Schenectady offices. Oriental rugs enhanced delicate antique furniture and the exquisitely framed paintings on the walls.

These surroundings, in turn, were in stark contrast to the BBDO quarters in New York City. The door from BBDO's no-nonsense reception room poured one into a sea of eye-high partitions that swelled relentlessly toward the walled horizon. Literally, it was a bullpen that would set to drooling the head of GE drafting in the quarter-mile long turbine building in Schenectady.

It became apparent in the first meeting with BBDO that the agency could marshall any amount of talent for the consumer portion of Live Better . . . Electrically, but very little for the traditional specialties of A&SP. There did not appear to be any seasoned cadres of people for press relations, for definitive brochures or How-To manuals, and the like. They did bring forth a single elderly gent who represented their exhibit expertise, but LBE elected to fall back on A&SP for certain functional needs, such as exhibits which A&SP handled at that time with more than 20 people, including planners, designers and buyers, plus a construction crew backed by a workshop and storage warehouse.

"Something wonderful happens . . ."

The creative team pulled together by BBDO for the initial recommended program of time and space was a thing of wonder.

BBDO outnumbered LBE by three to one. Seven BBDOers led us through the logic of market perspective, target demographics, media analysis, reach, frequency and whatnot until, at the end, we viewed the comp layouts and storyboards like old friends arriving for a reunion.

The creative director's presentation generated a couple of blips on the review screen. He preceded the unveiling of the ads with a 45-minute rationale on their execution. This left lingering doubts as to their effectiveness, because it was obvious there was no space in the ad to spell out the subliminal meaning, and he certainly couldn't go along to tell the story for each reader. And the proposed ad headline, "Something wonderful happens when you Live Better . . . Electrically," meant that the viewer still had to dig to find out what that something was. It took some polishing to put the ads and spots in order.

The conduct of the BBDO attendee sitting next to me matched the business mood of the office. This genial gentleman, introduced simply as Charlie Brower, listened casually, spoke infrequently, and spent a great deal of time tinkering with an LBE give-away I carried with me – an electric cigarette lighter.

Charlie Brower: "Pleasantly conspicuous"

It was obvious the CEO of BBDO was not out to impress anyone. He perfectly represented one of his notable quotes: "Honesty is not only the best policy, it is rare enough today to make you pleasantly conspicuous." His old-shoe conduct also reflected some of the taciturnity of Bruce Barton who, when lured to the agency world from writing, had stipulated he would "only work half days, do nothing but write, and not have to attend meetings, call on clients, hire or fire anyone, sign checks, or listen to lawyers or accountants."

Live Better . . . Electrically was hugely successful, exceeding all goals envisioned by GE for increased use of electricity, or load. That, in turn, expanded the market for all kinds of electrical equipment. For the first time, every segment of the industry could both participate in and enjoy the benefits of an integrated promotional thrust. And GE, of course, not only savored the taste of a larger slice of a much larger market pie, but again gained genuine credit for industry leadership.

Largely through the efforts of A&SP's Bob Ingmire, LBE sprouted a highly popular and productive offshoot called the Medallion Home program. Utilities awarded homeowners, literally, two kinds of medallions to affix on their front door frames: a gold one for those who modernized their homes with new wiring and lighting and all-electric appliances, plus heating and air conditioning, and a bronze medallion for those who converted all but the heating and cooling, in homes or apartments.

Many of the original program backers, including LBE staffers, scoffed at the thought that GE could entice its competitors to tie into an effort, industry-wide or not, that everyone knew had been spearheaded by General Electric. One staffer, in fact, bet me a dinner of choice that A&SP could never pull it off.

Biggest ever: 30 pages in *LIFE*

Perhaps the best proof of success was the promotional centerpiece for the Medallion Home program, a 30-page, one million dollar insert placed in *LIFE* magazine in September of 1959, as of that time the largest consumer ad ever placed in the U.S. It included extensive "editorial" in the distinctive *LIFE* format, prepared by our A&SP team, including Karl Koss, who now consults for GE corporate TV shows, Jim Clark, who manages GE educational communication programs in Fairfield, Walt Brzoza, now retired, and Bob Muir, who has his own agency in Manhattan. The insert featured not only ads by the various GE participants but those from Westinghouse, Sylvania, Thermador, Frigidaire, Kelvinator, Whirlpool, Owens Corning, Kennecott Copper, etc., as well.

The pay-off dinner in New York City was outstanding. And *very* expensive.

The waves from LBE created, in turn, ripples of varying ferment. At least half a dozen GE people claimed credit for the concept, and another three for the theme words. Art directors from both A&SP and BBDO vehemently vouched for paternity of the logo. In fact, it was originally designed by the latter and modified by the former, to the credit of both.

To this day, one can still see on the side of utility trucks in various parts of the country the familiar LBE logo, with a sunburst of artificial light emanating from a stylized house, framing a typical father, mother and child.

The view from *Mad* magazine and Tom Edison

The ultimate recognition, maybe, came from *Mad* magazine, which spoofed LBE with a satire on Die Better . . . Electrically. References to the electric chair and defense products such as the electrical Gatling gun developed by GE for aircraft flowed naturally from the pen. Fortunately, the magazine didn't know about a film tucked away in the GE archives.

Tom Edison had some people from A&SP make the film to illustrate the advantages of dc power, which he first favored, over ac power, which he later accepted as more practical. In one sequence, he applied current to an elephant. The poor beast stiffly jumped six inches off the floor, shuddered visibly, then crashed on its side to expire in a cloud of dust. The film was never widely released.

With LBE perking along nicely on its own in 1956, A&SP General Manager Rallie Reid proposed an intriguing new assignment for me: become GE's personal PR representative for a well-known Hollywood actor, Ronald Reagan, and accompany him on a tour of GE plants, fulfilling one segment of his role as television host of the GE Theatre. During the previous two years that Reagan had been associated with GE, this PR function had been carried out by Earl Dunckel, also from A&SP.

The prospect was intriguing because, according to Dunckel, a fundamental change was under way, changing Reagan the actor into Reagan the politician. That transformation was described by ex-GEer Edward Langley in a *New York Daily News* syndicated article:

> "GE people changed Reagan. Year after year, in smoky factories, he let himself be fork-lifted into the air to jabber with welders, or he bounded onto cafeteria tables to talk with clerks. In the beginning he tried to woo them with Hollywood jokes. But they weren't buying. They wanted, and in time forced him, to hear and respond to their concerns, their growls against government.
>
> "A lady coil winder hit him with 'Do you know how many licenses I need to open a part-time beauty parlor in my house? The government is running my life. Why?' A reluctant Reagan listened. He was nose-to-nose with middle America – and changing in the process. No other politician I can think of has been so steeped in the native conservatism of working America ... In seven years, he was so won over to working America that he began giving sizzling speeches to community groups that embarrassed his GE bosses, and they fired him."

Dear Ronald Reagan: Thanks, but no thanks

Since the Reagan job offer brought a great deal of suitcase living along with the territory, I declined. Also, maybe Reagan was ready to get out of show biz, but I wasn't.

He finally made the break, of course, and that ended his association with GE. As BBDO's Phil Dusenberry wryly noted in 1981 while the agency was gearing up for a new season of the GE Theatre, "We tried to get him this time around, but he wasn't available."

The glitter of the Big Time in the Big Agency by way of LBE dimmed somewhat when I arrived back in Schenectady. My old office was empty and my desk parked in the hallway.

No need to get excited, said Rallie. "The company is expanding and so is A&SP." It was a small symptom of things to come.

VI

REACHING OUT

❧

Won't it be nice, I thought, as I made a side trip on my way to San Jose, to let Phoenix know that all of the services of A&SP are available to the newly formed Computer Department. But the first thing I saw as I walked into the ad manager's office was a printed sign on the wall behind his desk which read: "We don't give a damn how they do it in Schenectady."

As GE took aim at the '50s, planners predicted that electrical manufacturing would grow at twice the rate of industry. Management, therefore, began to put in place building blocks that would shore up and enlarge GE's market share. The process re-shaped the profile of the company and, along the way, changed forever the tidy, traditional world of A&SP.

One cornerstone was research, from which would come products to fuel the planned growth. GE R&D investment had leaped three times beyond the average of other U.S. manufacturers and, in fact, led the list of them all. GE had a spanking new corporate R&D center in Schenectady, put up in 1950, and more than 100 back-up labs in product departments.

Marketing takes the lead

Decentralization rested firmly on the keystone over the front door – GE's new concept of marketing. It now positioned the function – in a move that was revolutionary at the time – at the beginning of the cycle instead of its traditional place at the end.

Integral to that process was communications, illustrated so well by the charter given A&SP to launch Live Better . . . Electrically.

GE also added on, in 1956, a game room – its new Management Research and Development Institute at Crotonville, NY, to bring the corporate gospel to aspiring new managers. On occasion inmates were tempted to equate it with another well-known institution just up the river, at Sing Sing. In time, however, they came to think of it affectionately as the "monastery with a bar."

GE growth following World War II had come largely from within. In the mid-'50s, GE began to take aim at "new, high cost technologies" it felt were essential to its new strategy. The prospects were exciting – in potential returns, in stepping beyond long-established bounds of electrical technology, and in literally building a new GE.

It was a time of change at GE, a time of reaching out, of trying things new.

The most obvious change showed up on the organization chart, in a dizzying array of new boxes. Many were vigorous off-shoots of established product businesses – turbines, transformers, motors, and the like.

Ordinarily, such expansion would have been contained within old-line anchor plants. But these no longer served as suitable relief valves. They had become bloated from the Korean War build-up; this had pumped up GE defense sales to almost a third of the company's total, tying up half its scientists. The plants were old, inefficient, and saddled with a recalcitrant work force.

The spin-offs reflected sizes and types of equipment that promised to mature on their own into new businesses. And this they soon nicely did, doubling the 138 GE plants in place in 1955 over little more than a decade.

As GE thrust these businesses beyond the walls of the old factory fortresses, the company marked its expanding frontiers with a series of cinderblock outposts, mainly in the cornfields of the midwest and the soft hills of the southeast.

The new plants, while still a part of the company, seemed more like independent fiefdoms, each tied by only two taut strings to headquarters – an overview of profit bogeys and of investment dollars.

Otherwise, these new product departments pretty much went their own way, engendering pride bordering on arrogance, from the general manager on down. Marketing, sales and ad managers were no exception, as A&SP soon found out.

Industry control in Salem, Virginia, flirted with the idea of doing an ad with – horrors! – a local agency. The General Purpose Control Department in Bloomington, Illinois, allowed as how it was going to pull out of the basic GE product handbook system – blasphemy! – and print its own catalog. Things were obviously getting out of hand.

A&SP branches out

A tentative response came in 1954 when A&SP opened two branch offices – both on a trial basis – in LaGrange, Illinois, and Winston-Salem, North Carolina. The troops were amazed to find there was indeed a world beyond Schenectady, and that such moves made good sense for both agency and client. Shortly, ad managers began to show up in Planning Board, and names like Shelbyville and Danville and Morrison and Hickory began to roll off the tongue as smoothly as Philadelphia and Lynn and Pittsfield.

While A&SP's fortunes were fashioned by the splintering of old businesses, they were strongly influenced by a proliferation of new ones. Many of these businesses grew out of work done by GE during World War II and the Korean War, ultimately coalescing in a new company group called Electronic, Atomic and Defense Systems.

One new business was foretold in 1954 when GE proudly unveiled its Network Analyzer, a huge panelboard bristling with dials, meters and interconnecting cables. For utilities, GE boasted it "cuts calculating time in half" when planning power systems. A year later, GE formed a new Computer Section – one step below product department status – and asked a study team to figure out what to do with its electronics business conglomerate.

Atomic power heats up

It seemed pretty obvious, too, that GE's atomic scope would soon go beyond the charter of national defense. The base was substantial – a plutonium-producing facility operated for the Atomic Energy Commission at Richland, Washington, along with the Knolls Atomic Power Laboratory in Schenectady where GE designed prototype submarine reactors, again for the A.E.C. And in a series of annual reports, beginning in 1951, GE noted cryptically it was "working on an atomic-powered aircraft engine."

Atomic energy was exactly the kind of natural bridge that GE sought to cross from defense to promising commercial ventures. After all, a reactor was nothing more than a source of heat which could replace the one big item in a power plant that GE didn't already make – the boiler. The business potential was exponential.

So beginning in 1954, A&SP began stopping off at a rented warehouse on Campbell Avenue in Schenectady to track a small band of people who were staking out GE's commercial future in atomic energy. The initial orders – some spec sheets and a slide presentation or two – didn't amount to much. But ex-A&SPer Ed McClure (now head of McClure & Associates Consulting in Stamford, CT), then one of the key ad people in the embryonic product department, assured us things would soon heat up.

A&SP also began dropping in on another key player, Dave Jones, who was later to join A&SP. He served as a sort of right-handyman for the newly appointed GE vice president of atomic power, Frank McCune, in Schenectady. As such, Jones became a mother hen for GE's atomic communications, both defense and commercial – preparing speeches for McCune, PR, testimony for the A.E.C., congressional briefings, articles, etc. What the job really entailed, Dave said, was "writing 265 pieces with a different view on the same subject."

The commercial end of the business heated up quickly, as McClure had predicted. GE began work in 1955 on the world's largest all-nuclear power plant for Commonwealth Edison in Chicago. Concurrently, the atomic business planted new roots in San Jose, California, building the world's largest private atomic laboratory at Vallecitos. It included an experimental power reactor which received the U.S. government's first operating license. By 1958, the business was blooming with almost 15,000 employees in both commercial and defense arenas.

Serving San Jose from Schenectady

A&SP ties with San Jose were so close that in the early years account servicing was launched from Schenectady. Account and creative people made the long haul – eight hours or so each way in pre-jet prop planes – every couple of months, staying a week or more at a time.

A&SP promoted the wares of San Jose in every conceivable medium, from direct mail to exhibits, from signed articles to periodicals, from space advertising to presentations for the Atomic Industrial Forum . . . even with comic books and a best-selling consumer motion picture, "A Is For Atom."

A&SP writers soon learned the language of loading fuel, going critical, "scramming" a reactor (forcing control rods in the core to stop a chain reaction), containment vessels, and so on. The last were dome-shaped housings surrounding power-producing equipment which could contain any radiation that might be released. One felt a proper sense of awe inside the reactor housing at Vallecitos, until technicians came by, hauling test instruments in a child's red wagon: an elegant engineering solution, and a comfort to those of us who felt nervous about getting so close to the cutting edge of technology.

A&SP art director John Watrous prevented one atomic engineer from toppling over the edge. The engineer had sent source drawings for a two-page, four-color ad featuring a cutaway of Commonwealth's Dresden Atomic Power Station. Watrous had rendered countless cutaways of GE fossil-fueled turbines, so he sent back word that unless the turbine supports were strengthened, upon start-up the utility would wind up with a hundred tons of precision metal in the basement. The drawings were promptly altered.

By 1958, San Jose had orders on the books for 18 reactors. Two thirds were for pint-sized test reactors with the rest small, power-producing plants. It appeared that once again GE would have to galvanize utilities into the big end of this emerging market and, if everything worked right, gain share along the way.

So that same year in Woodside, California at the third Electric Utility Excutives Conference, produced and staged by A&SP, GE proposed a two-phase program to accelerate the development of atomic power, heretofore almost exclusively the domain of the federal government.

Operation Sunrise

The first phase, Operation Sunrise, called for utilities to construct five medium-size developmental plants that could lead the way to competitive nuclear power by 1965. The second phase, Operation Know-How, proposed that each utility put in place a small power reactor of its own, like the GE unit at Vallecitos, to show people that atomic plants were really good neighbors.

A&SP mounted a massive market development effort, bringing to bear the full spectrum of communications to solicit support from electric utilities, the government, industry influence groups, security analysts, and the considerable group of GE people concerned with atomic energy.

"Sunrise" was moderately successful, gaining a couple of plant orders in the target range. The reception for "Know-How," on the other hand, was anything but nuclear. It was as if someone had scrammed the control rods into the core argument. The response was almost wholly negative. In retrospect, this lack of interest on the part of utilities may have been the single biggest miscalculation ever made by them in regard to their future.

A&SP, in close cooperation with Dave Jones and the San Jose ad group headed by H. A. "Bud" Beaudoin, had monitored some disquieting developments on the news front. More and more, in the press and on the air, people scripted scare scenarios, equating atomic power with worst-case radiation, and "the bomb." The escalating tempo sounded a clear warning to the industry. It appeared, however, that with quick action we might muffle, if not contain, the concerns.

"Citizen Atom"

Accordingly A&SP, along with Jones and the San Jose group, proposed to atomic top management in the Spring of 1960 that GE spearhead an industry-wide, public understanding program called "Citizen Atom." This would tell people how beneficial atomic power could be in cost, cleanliness, safety, etc. The story would be beamed via a three-pronged, multi-million dollar program – directly to the public, directly to influence groups, and indirectly to the public through influence groups.

The initial reaction from Lyman "Tiny" Fink, who had taken over as vice president of the Atomic Products Division, was encouraging: "Last Sunday, my minister preached that we should spend our money on good things, not atomic bombs. Your timing is perfect."

Then practicality set in. George White, general manager of the commercial atomic business operation, responded sadly: "We may sink if they keep loading expenses on us." And Fink got tangled up in timing – "Is it too soon, or too late?" He bounced the program up the line to higher management for a reinforcing reading and got nothing but reverberations. The program never made it, as we had proposed, to the president, Bob Paxton, nor to Cordiner, who had strongly supported the "Know-How" concept.

"Gents, we're clutching burlap"

Instead, "Citizen Atom" caromed back to Fink, who decided he could only spare $100,000. This, of course, meant a drastic scaling down of objectives for our A&SP team. As Joe Morton, the wry mid-midwestern representing the news bureau, observed: "Gents, we're clutching burlap."

A&SP did manage to squeeze out a 16-page supplement in *The New York Times,* reinforced by the sale of nearly a million reprints, plus self-liquidating film kits for schools and public interest groups, a travelling exhibit, and so on.

The team had comforting facts to spread: scientists had proved that one gets less radiation living next door to an atomic power plant than from the natural radiation in a brick house. A San Jose scientist displayed his faith in a GE atomic plant by drinking the discharge water from one.

A Schenectady GE scientist, Henry Hurwitz, Jr., documented later that the maximum public exposure from the Three Mile Island incident was only 40% of the legal limit for a nuclear facility during a whole year. He also noted that the EPA's "safe" cumulative exposure for indoor radon occurring naturally in a typical house each year is about the same as the exposure of the Chernobyl evacuees in Russia – i.e., 16 to 32 times more than the legal lifetime public exposure from a U.S. nuclear plant.

But these were drops of reason in a flood of angry words. The now-familiar cycle of protest and delay gained momentum every year, effectively cancelling out the most promising way utilities had ever had to get fuel costs and availability under firm control.

Turnkey or turkey?

For a while, it appeared that GE's nuclear business might make it big anyway. The company knew that utilities were greatly influenced by the herd instinct. So, in hope of starting a stampede, GE offered – a first by any supplier – firm prices and warranties on "turnkey" atomic power plants.

This had precisely the desired effect – big plant orders soared. Things looked so good that in 1964, A&SP opened an office in San Jose to handle the fallout in communications. The only problem was that the mounting turmoil of protests and delays sent plant costs sky high, with GE left holding the bag. It may have been the "Coming of Age" of the nuclear power business, as GE proudly proclaimed in 1965, but it would be 10 more years before it became even marginally profitable, and then at a time when plant cancellations began to top new orders.

A&SP's San Jose contingent, like the rest of the nuclear people there, sustained themselves during the period by promoting fuel and services. Ads touted zirconium (which was good for your reactor) and "crud" (which was bad). GE would be glad to deliver the former, and clean out the latter.

Even so, the business never really recovered, and the future looks no better. Poignant reminders of the Citizen Atom program underscore why. In the 1976 annual report, GE noted that the future growth of nuclear power will depend on "favorable public acceptance." As late as December 1986, the Senior Vice President of GE's Power Systems Business, Jack Urquhart, wistfully noted that "the nuclear option" must overcome the impediment of "a more rational understanding by the public of the advantages and disadvantages of nuclear power."

While GE's atomic business had attained an orders backlog of $6.2 billion by 1975, even that paled in the light of the prospects for another new business venture: computers.

The object of the reach was IBM. GE gave top priority to getting in on some of the action with one of the fastest growing companies in the world, in one of the fastest growing industries.

GE's Jim Baker, senior vice president of the Industrial Sector, once noted that more than half the members of the Fortune 500 slid off the list between 1945 and 1970, adding, "It's lonely up there with all those oil companies." The pace set by IBM as it rocketed up the scale threatened not only to dispel any loneliness in GE, but also to surpass the company. Of course, IBM soon did, but it's tailed off badly of late due to problems in pricing and market share.

IBM: "Oh boy, here they come!"

GE's start in computers was inauspicious. Its early work on analog computers by engineers down deep in the labs had led to rudimentary digital computers for industrial systems, home territory for GE. Then in 1950, some of these people came up with a data processing concept for business. A year later, GE sold several computer systems based on this concept to the Bank of America, and launched a network of information processing centers. This opened the door into IBM's realm only a crack. But, according to rumor, it was enough to prompt Tom Watson to say: "Oh boy, here they come!"

A&SP opportunities in computers were pretty much what it had found in other areas where it had no filial or organizational ties. Initial calls by A&SP on the marketing manager and ad manager, were rebuffed – they were quite happy with local service and with their agency in Los Angeles, thank you very much. Schenectady's view of all this: what can you expect from 30 bearded people in funny string ties and cowboy boots who mill around a rented office all day in a hick town like Phoenix?

A&SP did pick up an odd job now and then. The L.A. agency writers didn't understand utilities, so we did a brochure on a GE process computer system for Southern California Edison. Phoenix couldn't figure out how to persuade their sales force to hand out to customers a huge stock of symbolic giveaways – a slide rule, representing analog, and an abacus, for digital. We suggested they stock them in the A&SP warehouse in Schenectady and put a price on them to denote value. In two months, the salesmen cleared the shelves.

A&SP also put together some sales kits for the information processing centers, headquartered in Schenectady. But over-all, the prospects were desolate.

Byte by byte, the odds improve

Suddenly, the game changed when the players changed. In mid 1965, a long time A&SPer, Dick Gleason, left to become ad manager of the Computer Department in Phoenix. He promptly announced that he intended to bring A&SP on scene.

Prospects brightened even more next year when another familiar name surfaced as the new general manager of the Information Systems Division – A&SP's old boss, J. Stanford Smith. He sprinkled ex-A&SPers throughout his entourage, including Ken Yarbrough, who seemed to roam the organization as a pipeline to and from Smith, and John Callihan (now vice president of public relations for Westvaco), who directed marketing communications from the division level.

Less than a year later, A&SP opened a Phoenix office and mounted several fully integrated communication programs in support of GE's rapidly expanding lines. The business, which had blossomed from well below 100 people to more than 3,000 in just five years, sprouted small computers from Olivetti in Italy, medium range systems from Machines Bull in France, optical readers from Philadelphia, Medinet systems for hospitals from Boston, components from Oklahoma City, and so forth. Ad series touted the marketing theme, GE "Compatibles," as well as the flexibility of computer time-sharing through GE information processing centers. Testimonial ads for the latter were a natural, because GE had lined up ventures with such computer pioneers as Bell Labs, MIT, and Dartmouth College, the latter through its work in developing Basic computer language, under the direction of John G. Kemeny, who later became Dartmouth's president.

Phoenix chose a natural way to beam its message to top

executives throughout industry: sponsorship of TV golf tournaments. When Smith casually mentioned plans for an upcoming commercial to Gerald Phillippe, GE's chairman at the time, the latter seemed incredulous. "Golf? The only ones who watch that are people like me." (Pause) "Oh."

In an effort to put the growing computer complex in focus for the customer, A&SP prepared an identification guidebook that established a common format and symbol for all components to use in worldwide communications. To the extent it was feasible within GE, it worked – ranging beyond ads and print materials to everything from trade signs to jewelry. It still ranked a distant second to IBM, which had long found it not only feasible but mandatory to create an IBM "look." This went far beyond ads to architectural design and the dress of its starchy sales people.

A&SP's ride with the computer business was exhilarating. For a while, it looked like GE might give IBM a real run for the money. By 1969, the company had acquired five product lines, fielded more than 8,000 people from 13 locations in five countries, and installed $1.3 billion of equipment, including 3,000 small scale systems.

"Oh boy, there they go!"

That same year, Smith moved on to head up the International Group. It still looked like GE was in the computer business to stay. Based upon what the company had said time and time again, there did not appear to be any way GE could get out of it – "systems" were at the heart of GE's business, and computers were at the heart of those systems.

And so in 1970, Tony Turner labored in the A&SP Phoenix office on copy for a new brochure entitled "Commitment to the Industry," when word came down that the business had been sold to Honeywell.

Actually, the sale didn't mean the death-knell for GE's commitment to the systems concept. While it sold its business computers, the company held on to some systems equipment – process computers, which were sold four years later, and both aerospace computers and its data communications business, which it kept.

Beating the system

GE systems engineers had long been a potent force in reaching out for new business – and they represented an invaluable resource for A&SP. The best of the application engineers, sophisticated yet pragmatic, literally lived with customers and often knew the industry better than those they served. When A&SP people were ready to initiate strategy for a new program, they would go to Building 2 to talk to Ted Rich, who was "Mr. Cement," or to George Shaad, who was "Mr. Paper," or to the other experts across the board. The proper starting point in the marketing process – the customer – was second nature with GE application engineers, and it rubbed off on A&SPers.

The GE systems business served up the kind of stories that let A&SP honestly position GE out front of the competitive pack. There were computer integrated control systems for whole power plants, and the same for industrials, such as the industry first at McLouth Steel. There were large GE power control rooms built and tested in the factory, then plopped into place on the floor of a customer's factory. There was also GE's vision of the "Ring of Automation," which allowed one to move foward a step at a time toward a GE concept that later promised the "Factory with a Future."

GE's systems engineering business was pretty much broken up in the late '70s, but not before A&SP coined a theme for a major ad program in *Business Week*: Engineered Industrial Systems. While the function diminished, "engineered" retained a lure that set the scientists and engineers a-fluttering – probably more inside the company than without. The phrase kept popping up all over the place – engineered materials, engineered castings, engineered drives, engineered solutions, and so on.

The company's outreach during these years strongly affected two other promising areas: major appliances in Louisville, and plastics in Pittsfield.

Live Better . . . Electrically had helped stimulate a major resurgence in consumer demand in the late '50s, and appliance sales swelled as one part of the GE package offered through the Medallion Home program. From the original target – homeowners – the marketing and sales guns swivelled to multi-dwelling building contractors, then later to total electric communities, nurtured by a new GE Construction Market Development Operation.

It became obvious that if A&SP didn't extend itself, its lot in Louisville would routinely be the bits and pieces that spilled out from Medallion Home days. In 1964, therefore, it swallowed hard – Louisville still retained the view of A&SP as a pesky sibling – and opened an office, with Dick Huether in charge. Business picked up right away in A&SP's target niche – not consumer time and space, but collateral for the service and dealer support functions, so important to that business.

A&SP also made some tentative stabs at GE plastics, which kept devising exotic new materials. For example, A&SP tacked its name on the bidding list to propose a program for a promising new material called PPO. This had been developed in the nearby hamlet of Selkirk, home of a hard driving young GE engineer named Jack Welch. Results of the competitive ad program review, however, came from a newly hired marketing trainee, who turned A&SP down. After a few more desultory probes with no better results, A&SP gave up for the time being.

GE marketers discover the world

About this time, GE marketing people discovered the world. They were surprised to find that various other GE people had been prospecting abroad for years, primarily application engineers.

The communications problem lay in getting a firm grip on the company's presence internationally, and what it had to offer. The message was a confused jumble of exported goods, overseas plants, joint ventures, reps, licensees, and what not – it was left to the customer to put things in focus. A great many people overseas, therefore, looked on GE as did the man in the famous McGraw-Hill house promotion ad. He confronted the salesman with: "I don't know who you are; I don't know your company; I don't know your company's product; I don't know what your company stands for; etc., etc. Now, what was it you wanted to sell me?"

A&SP set out to enhance the view of its growing international business through various programs. Buford Barr initiated one effort in 1973, and another, directed by Bob Ingmire, lobbed a series of ads covering a complex range of GE industrial goods, translated into native tongues to match country media. A later program, aimed at developing nations, proffered the claim that "GE gives you the power to energize an infrastructure," and almost anything else in the world. There was no way management could fault this program: A&SP's Frank Paul developed an integrated program matrix which intertwined with the strategic business plan of GE's International Sales Divison.

Building a forum for world leaders

Actually, A&SP had backed into the international arena earlier through a GE publication called the *Defense Quarterly*. The periodical was conceived by A&SPers Gene Bradley, Dave Jones and

Roy Stratton, and was sponsored by defense-oriented product departments. This led to a second publication called the *GE Forum* which was just that – it featured articles by such world leaders as presidents Kennedy, Johnson and Ford, and by Henry Ford, Harvey Firestone, Peter Drucker, C. P. Snow, Henry Cabot Lodge, James Doolittle, and Chester Bowles. The last made it not because of a distinguished career in advertising (chairman of Benton & Bowles), but as U.S. Ambassador to India.

GE Forum, which was later edited by A&SP's Bill Hickman, proved to be, as noted by an aide to GE Chairman Reginald Jones, "our one regular contact with the power centers and executive offices of the United States."

No one in A&SP was surprised, then, when editor Bradley cabled from Europe where he strove to line up authors: "Can't get Churchill. How about DeGaulle?" Nor was his wife taken aback in the least when, on calling upstairs to Gene in their home that a Mr. Dulles was on the phone, Gene answered with a perfectly straight face: "Which one?" This was during the Eisenhower administration; John Foster Dulles was Secretary of State and his brother, Allan, was Director of the CIA.

In the late '60s, when the company's international sales began climbing steeply toward $2 billion, A&SP made a full commitment to the market. Reid chartered the news bureau's Jim McGarry to set up a beachhead in Europe, manned by A&SP veterans: Jim Baar in Paris, Jim Hurley in Frankfurt, Bob Jones in London, and Peter Tarantelli in Milan. They quickly formed alliances with leading local agencies and began pumping out a respectable flow of marketing communications and PR. However, the volume never built up enough to sustain the overhead, and the troops were withdrawn in 1970.

While home base reverted to Schenectady, A&SP staffers continued to roam the world in support of served accounts. Sometimes A&SP focused on pure selling, preparing a string of brochures on electric vehicle control translated for use in Europe. Again, the primary need shifted to image-building, preparing the way for Australian GE to push motor starters.

The Exhibit Operation was particularly active – presenting the wares of 32 GE product businesses before 200,000 Chinese at a trade show in Peking; shipping 30 tons of displays for a Science and Technology Exhibition in Saudi Arabia; even flitting in and out of Baghdad between bombings to participate in a trade fair, at a time when Iraq had no diplomatic relations with the U.S.

Much of this reflected the great pressure GE exerted on all components to probe likely new areas of business. In one case, A&SP worked closely with the U.S. network of GE Apparatus Service Shops as it moved to repair *any* kind of heavy equipment, not just that made by GE. The network expanded beyond the U.S., encompassing almost 200 shops in 19 countries. To make sure overseas shop managers didn't have to start from scratch in putting together their communication programs, A&SP developed a "Promotions Made Easy" matrix, based on unsophisticated, literal "building block" promotional and selling aids.

While A&SP's European mission was discouraging, it didn't deter General Manager Reid from devising another strategy that mirrored the target of the Service Shops: non GE-related business.

A&SP had informally tested the outside waters briefly through a kind of consortium under section manager Jack Dumas, again in the late '60s. Jerry Perazzo – assisted by Chuck Matzell, longtime outside art director and consultant Charlie Hepburn, and Bill Berg on production – gained some fun-type consumer business: Green Stamps, Diner's Club, GE's Radio Receiver Department (radio and TV commercials), and even the in-flight magazine for Mohawk Airlines, later swallowed up by Allegheny/USAir.

Selling outside GE: MCI

This activity was swept into a new A&SP organization called MCI, for Marketing Communications International. The director was Jim Baar, who later left GE to become senior VP for PR with Hill & Knowlton in Boston, and then president of Creamer Dickson Basford, Inc. in Providence. He and a few associates, including Jim Hurley (now senior consultant with the Tidewater Group in Stamford, CT), enlisted all the account people in A&SP to devote a portion of their time selling A&SP services outside the company. Everybody experienced a phenomenal, immediate gain in stature, at least on their new MCI business cards: to Group Executive, which at the time was the top layer of operating management in GE.

As a first step, Baar and Hurley picked up the Utica Club beer account, a refreshing change from the dreary, old-line GE apparatus accounts. But they intended to go beyond such froth and delve more deeply into businesses where A&SP could make a professional contribution.

One target, though marginal to the outside world, was a small, wholly owned GE subsidiary. MCI enthusiastically sold a major program, including as its centerpiece a $72,000 brochure. When this element was completed, reviewing management killed the venture: projected net income for the operation that year, before the brochure, was only $62,000.

Conflicts of interest

MCI soon faced a more formidable obstacle: commercial conflicts of interest. GE business activities were so diversified in so many places that it was almost impossible for MCI to chart a clear course.

My operation landed a small environmental manufacturing concern and we were well under way on their first campaign when word came down from Vice President Wells Corbin, A&SP's boss who headed GE Industrial Sales: Back off. Corporate R&D had a small group that was interested in the same business segment. We also had initiated talks with a very substantial area firm, Albany International, which had expressed an interest in going with MCI. Then we discovered one of their divisions made billiard balls – with their own plastic, not the competitive material available from GE – and that was the end of that.

The sobering fact was that MCI's market was riddled with holes, and the venture capitulated in advance of an almost certain collapse. But if nothing more, the MCI episode made a lot of us feel better, because it proved what many had long suspected: it's far easier to sell outside GE than within.

At the end of the '60s, then, A&SP lowered its sights to the comforting confines of GE. That in itself was world enough to keep anyone busy and challenged. And A&SP still had its various branch offices and eight news bureau outposts to take care of whatever came into sight.

Symbolically, the ending of the decade unfolded an opportunity for A&SP to display its proper stature – physically at least. Late in June of 1960, a tornado cut a swath through Schenectady, barely missing the GE plant. Then on July 7, Building 6 caught fire and was extensively damaged. For practical reasons, dictated by company policy, A&SP relocated most operations not in creditable new quarters befitting an agency but in nearby Building 23, where the company first made refrigerators, long ago.

The move didn't reinforce Leo Burnett's philosophy that if you "reach for the stars, at least you won't come up with a handful of mud." But it did offer A&SPers a priceless legacy for years to come.

It used to be that when one wanted to get away for whatever, one would say: "I'm stopping off at Maqua (A&SP's printing company) on the way home." Now, in addition, one could parry an infinite range of questions about work that went astray with the retort: "Beats me. Must have burned in the Bldg. 6 fire."

VII

FLAK SUITS

"By God!" said Bill Ginn, GE's vice president for turbines, as he slammed his fist on the layout I had just presented, "I'm going to cut out this advertising once and for all!" This didn't make sense to me, since all of his turbine marketing managers had heartily endorsed the campaign. Then the price-fixing scandal of 1960 came to light, and I understood.

One of A&SP's major missions, as with any communications agency, was to build a strong, positive image for clients. With GE this meant not only the various served components, but the company as a whole.

Most of the time, this was easy; you felt you had integrity on your side. As *The New York Times* once reported, GE "had always taken it as a given."

Appliances also gave the company a strong household presence that helped it rise above "unsavory publicity," as Prof. John Fleming of the University of Southern California School of Graduate Business Administration noted, in *The Wall Street Journal*: "Their products work well and are reliable. GE has a good image."

A&SP traded heavily on these strengths, in all forms of communications. And, always, A&SP kept in mind that they were a legacy from earlier days, and had been carefully nurtured. Reputation is fragile and fleeting.

GE brought to bear every communications tool at its disposal to sustain this favorable image. In its first true corporate ad in 1916, for example, the company ignored products and instead documented GE's dedication to a better quality of life through electricity. Soon thereafter, the company sought to inspire its employees, too, through an internal magazine called the *Monogram,* which began a series of monthly reports – continuing to this day – on the aims and achievements of GE people.

Early GE institutional campaigns included the classic corporate ad produced by Bruce Barton (the second B in BBDO), headlined "The Initials of a Friend," illustrated by a large GE logo. It became the prototype for hundreds of similar GE ads spanning a seven year period, in a series called Building an Electrical Consciousness.

Floyd Gibbons and the House of Magic

As radio became more popular in the 1920s and '30s, GE initiated a new corporate show called The General Electric Hour. In a departure from convention, the company signed on a fast-talking, one-eyed newscaster named Floyd Gibbons to do the commercials.

Gibbons' treatment of wide-ranging developments going on in GE was, appropriately, electric. His broadcasts crackled with the excitement of inventions coming out of the GE corporate R&D Lab in Schenectady, which he dubbed the House of Magic. This became the theme for the GE exhibits at the Chicago and New York World's Fairs in 1933 and 1939-40; corporate then packaged the performances into highly successful road shows. While it's hard to conceive, requests to put on the House of Magic still came in during the late 1970s, more than 30 years after the last showing.

While communications tools aided in building a positive image, GE depended even more on the skills of its people. The one individual who probably did more than any other to add lustre to the GE monogram was Clyde D. Wagoner. He had fashioned the news bureau out of the old Publicity Department back in the 1920s, and was just completing a distinguished career there when I joined the component in 1954 for an A&SP tour of duty.

To those who didn't bother to delve beneath the surface, Wagoner appeared to be nothing more than an old time press agent . . . maybe the last of the lot. But this was no act. This was the real thing.

Wag, as everyone called him, looked the part. He always wore his hat at work. A slight man, he would hunch forward in his formal suit at an old upright typewriter, stare intently through and beyond the cigarette that was constantly in his hand, and tap out stories. Both those he wrote and those he told were fascinating.

I discovered with amazement that Wag represented a direct link with Thomas Edison and Charles P. Steinmetz, dating back to early GE days. He remembered both well, because they had been his news beat.

News beat: Tom Edison

Covering Edison, according to Wag, wasn't easy. The inventor's associates, he told me, didn't want anyone to interfere with Edison's work habits, which were legendary. "They said he kept hard at it for 20 hours straight every day and, as proof, showed me the working quarters in his laboratory where Edison had strung a blanket over a rope to shut out distractions.

"One day," continued Wag, "when his associates were elsewhere, I stuck my head around the blanket to plead my case for an interview. I quickly found that he was as mortal as the rest of us – he was taking a nap on a cot."

This quirk in the Edison legend brought to mind another anecdote related by the advertising pioneer Earnest Elmo Calkins, in his biography "and hearing not . . ." Both Calkins and Edison teetered on the edge of total deafness.

"We (Calkins & Holden) handled the Edison advertising many years. Anyone who knew Mr. Edison knew how little patience he had for communication by writing notes – or for that matter for communication of any kind. I once asked him why he, of all persons, did not avail himself of one of the many electrical devices for making hearing less difficult. His reply was characteristic: 'Too busy. A lot of time is wasted in listening. If I had one of those things my wife would want to talk to me all the time.' "

While Edison was more widely known, Wagoner nominated Steinmetz, the electrical genius who contributed so much to GE's technological stature, as his favorite contact. This partly stemmed from a fabulous memory.

Steinmetz hypes the turbine

When GE sold the first 60,000 kilowatt turbine, according to Wag, he asked Steinmetz if he could help him find a news hook to dramatize it. Without hesitation, the scientist said: "60,000 kilowatts is about 80,000 horsepower – and one horsepower is equivalent to the muscle power of 22 and one half men."

Steinmetz continued: "Since the turbine works 24 hours a day, while men work only eight hours, the 60,000 kilowatt turbine does the work of 5,400,000 men – more than could be done by all the slaves in the South before the Civil War."

Wag thought maybe he ought to check the library before writing his story, and discovered Steinmetz was right on target: in 1860, there were 4,700,000 slaves in the U.S.

Wag's accomplishments rested on a firmer base than antiquity. He understood the formula of the true press agent: it's OK to promote a point of view, but it's best done as a by-product of some dramatic news event that legitimately puts your company in the public eye.

How successful did he become?

Thanks, Clyde: Admiral Byrd

Down near the bitter tip of Antarctica, there's a peak officially named Mt. Clyde Wagoner. The famed explorer, U.S. Admiral Richard E. Byrd, designated it in gratitude for the GE short wave radio hookup which Wag arranged for Byrd's camp at Little America. Because of it, the homesick men could chat with their families back in the company's studios in Schenectady.

The service to Byrd was, of course, humanitarian. But Wag had something more in mind. Listeners all over the nation tuned in on the conversations with Little America, and this generated news stories throughout the world. As Wag expected, the company's name appeared prominently.

When Hitler began his threatening moves in the late 1930s, Wagoner again brought GE short wave into play to beam the American News Tower to Europe, with the approval of President Franklin D. Roosevelt. The format was used again during World War II, becoming the forerunner of the Voice of America.

Wag constantly created new ways to promote GE. He staged a tug of war between electric and steam locomotives – the former the winner and, of course, made by GE. He arranged the first radio drama and the first play-by-play broadcast of a football game. When GE's radio station WGY prepared to dedicate its new studio, Wag persuaded the Navy to fly one of its huge dirigibles over Schenectady and transmit a beam of light to officially put the facility on the air.

He also re-created the "shot heard 'round the world," lining up the governor of Massachusetts to fire a Revolutionary War musket so the sound, transmitted by cooperating short wave stations, would circle the globe. Actually, neither the governor

nor anyone else could get the musket to fire, so former A&SP head Chet Lang, now a vice president, fired a blank pistol instead. Being pre-TV, the audience never knew the difference.

Wanted: a dozen live flies

During one dreary stretch of winter, Wag ran an ad in New York City newspapers offering to pay for a dozen live flies. Reporters promptly gathered to see if he'd get any and, if so, what he intended to do with them. "Be patient," Wag told them. "Somebody's bound to show up."

Sure enough, a boy soon arrived with a cage full – he was raising them for a laboratory which tested insect sprays. And what did Wag want them for? He promptly brought out a new GE radio mike that was so sensitive, he said, that it could pick up a fly's footsteps. Which turned a routine new product announcement into an event that drew worldwide press coverage.

In Wagoner's time, as in later years, GE was immensely proud of its stature in U.S. councils of business and state. The company had long settled comfortably among the top 10 corporations of the *Fortune* 500. GE also hovered near the top of the nation's leading defense contractors, and headed the list of electrical equipment makers.

This penchant for pre-eminence paid off in many ways. GE gained more U.S. patents, year after year, than any other company in the world, including the Japanese. Its grip on quality was so consistent that the Gallup Poll of U.S. consumers, as late as 1985, placed GE at the head of the world's companies noted for the quality of their products and services.

Hawking free enterprise

As a counterpoint to its leadership in market development, GE staked out a strong position on major national issues, richly cloaked in the mantle of free enterprise. These provided natural springboards for A&SP to launch campaigns that reinforced corporate themes.

The company, according to a recurring lament of Cordiner, faced a "steadily mounting burden of taxes ... (which are) approaching confiscatory levels." So on behalf of its utility-oriented clients, A&SP created an ad headlined "Us and Taxes," which suggested "it is a tribute to American industry that manufacturers can remain competitive" when thirty-five cents of every dollar paid goes for taxes. For good measure, A&SP also prepared an ad for *The New York Times* lambasting New York State for spending taxpayer dollars on foreign-made hydro turbines, when domestic units (i.e., GE) were better, albeit costing more.

GE applauded when President Charlie Wilson was made U.S. Chief of Mobilization at the outbreak of the Korean conflict. Concurrently, the company devoted about 25% of its business to defense projects. So, locking into the corporate pace, A&SP prepared, on a regular basis, insertions such as the three-page ad in *LIFE* magazine in 1952 on "The fastest 10 years in history." This chronicled GE's development of jet engines which powered the world's fastest fighters and bombers and, soon thereafter, gained 18 of 25 world speed records for U.S. aircraft. A&SP also ran an ad series in *U.S. News & World Report* and the news weeklies documenting how GE subcontracting helped thousands of small firms participate in the defense of the nation.

"Tremblin' in the Kremlin"

The 1958 annual report trumpeted that, as a good corporate citizen, "GE is doing its share to help the United States respond vigorously to the Soviet bid for world leadership." At an executive customer conference, A&SP presented a dramatic skit called "Tremblin' in the Kremlin," which suggested that things under way at GE would give pause to the red menace.

In 1959, GE warned: "The next decade is one in which U.S. business enterprises must take into account not only the prospect of more vigorous competition among themselves, but also from competition abroad." So A&SP promptly solicited sponsorship of an ad series in *The Wall Street Journal* that proclaimed new ways to "Keep America Competitive."

Most times, A&SP comfortably followed the lead of the company in promoting positions through communications. But not always.

In the early '70s, for example, A&SP uneasily eyed a new theme coming down from corporate called "Men helping man," and wondered what to do with it. Fortunately, evolution solved the problem: somebody up there discovered women, and concluded that in spite of the generic intent of the words, the slogan was, in the current climate, indiscreet.

And then there were those few times when GE people became loose cannons, blowing big holes in the company's standard of ethical and moral leadership.

"The Incredible Electrical Conspiracy"

The most dramatic instance resulted in the anti-trust suits brought by the U.S. government in 1959 against GE and 29 other defendant companies. The incident was summed up by a headline in *Fortune* magazine: "The Incredible Electrical Conspiracy." Before it was over, it became the stimulus for one of the most memorable campaigns ever produced by A&SP.

It is true that GE, like other manufacturers, faced rough times in the late '50s. These arose from many of the things GE had railed against in position papers: chronic over-capacity, depressed prices, increasing foreign competition and, as usual, intense pressure from management to achieve targeted results. Through it all, the company seemed to remain at equilibrium. It maintained a steady ratio of market share to that of competition, apparently by selling quality and value.

Yet when the government announced its preliminary findings in 1959, it became obvious that high quality was outweighed by hanky panky. In ironic contrast to the messages GE had beamed to customers for so long, J. Cullen Ganey, Chief Judge of the U.S. District Court in Philadelphia, made it clear that "... what is really at stake here is the survival of the kind of economy under which this country has grown great, the free enterprise system."

Stretching back to 1958, a number of GE executives had conspired with their competitive peers to divvy up the utility market, fix prices, and rig bids to make sure each got an allotted share.

Selling by "phase of the moon"

Participants selected code numbers representing their companies. They attended meetings referred to as "choir practice." The jumble of prices was so complex that the Antitrust Division finally brought in a cryptographer in a fruitless search for a cartel pattern. Ultimately, testimony in the 1960 trials revealed why the code was so difficult to decipher – switchgear prices had been rigged, literally, according to the phases of the moon.

The shock waves from the scandal reverberated through A&SP as they did through the rest of the company. GE auditors sifted through A&SP expense accounts – particularly AVCOM people who had worked with the accused executives. The A&SP team calling on the switchgear account in Philadelphia concluded that chit-chat at adjoining tables in the plant's now infamous Dining Room D was likely not as idle as it had seemed. And a sizeable number of A&SPers discovered the campaigns they had so carefully prepared for turbines and transformers and switchgear and capacitors were wattless exercises. The buying pattern had been short-circuited by sellers.

The shock to utilities, of course, exceeded that of A&SP. Here was a GE market representing more than 10 per cent of total company sales. It was the very foundation upon which the company had been built. In one sharp ethical transgression, most of the GE management team calling on utilities disappeared, and traditionally close sales ties abruptly changed to arm's length transactions.

As if to underscore the problem, GE stock shed $684 million in paper value.

The cultural hemorrhage of anti-trust called for more than a simple PR bandage. Certain steps had to be taken, going beyond simply replacing the old utility sales management. The new people had to be introduced to customers who had freshly turned cynical. Three hundred and fifty sales engineers, responsible for contacts with 20,000 buying influences, badly needed new talking points to raise the tenor of their talk. Above all, the company desperately sought to re-establish its traditional thrust of industry leadership.

To A&SP: please fix

But even a good response wouldn't mean much if utilities didn't get the word. So the call came down to A&SP: mold us some ammunition for our marketing rifles and shotguns. And this, more of a command than a caveat: integrate what GE says, instead of the usual clatter that comes from 15 utility-oriented GE businesses singing their own songs in their own disparate ways.

A&SP had often formed small creative teams to map out strategy for major programs. But this one was different. Some 50 people representing almost every A&SP function convened on a Saturday to wrestle with the challenge during an all day session.

Recurringly, the discussion focused on a basic question: which way would lead to a mutually attractive future for utilities and GE?

The answer finally came from the head of the news bureau, Jim McGarry, who cut through the clutter to ask whimsically: "Whither?" Instantly, this became the theme for the campaign, as well as the headline for the kick-off ad. A sprinkling of violently colored arrows, pointing randomly, illustrated the total copy: "Which path will lead to vigorous growth and profitability for the electrical industry?"

Today, the ad appears deceptively simple . . . perhaps too much so. Yet in context with the typically ponderous trade ads of the time, or even those of today, it reflected a vitality that was unusual, even exciting for GE.

Whither? Hither

In quick succession, A&SP spewed forth new ideas via new GE ads: "Hither," with the arrows pointing uniformly to the enormous sales and load growth potential from all-electric high rise buildings; "Killing Time," an urgent call to do away with deadly smog through air-clearing electricity; "Going, going, gone," linking the descent of transformers from pole top to pad mount to underground, with a rise in environmental favor; "No, lady," featuring a bug-proof meter; and so on.

Later ads featured new members of GE management, new products, new areas of research, and new GE initiatives in making, delivering and using electricity. Advertising conformed to a common format and theme, from trade books to *The Wall Street Journal.* The strategy carried over into marketing and sales, as well as brochures, direct mail, films, speeches, press relations, and presentation materials, for use both with individuals and mass audiences.

The major spokesman for the campaign, in the ads and in personal initiatives, was C. K. "Chuck" Rieger, newly appointed vice president and group executive of GE's Electric Utility Group. He seemed the ideal choice for the job – boyish-looking yet erudite, fun-loving while authoritative. Rieger had most recently headed GE's consumer goods business. From that free-wheeling orientation, he relished the new A&SP ad campaign when it first thundered off the launching pad. Yet, as so often happens, he tired of it before there was any indication that customers did.

So he asked Bob Ingmire, who was heading up the account: "How about something new?" Bob, in turn, tossed the challenge to me.

In truth, I was a bit tired of the series, too, since we had churned out close to a hundred ads. Therefore, drawing upon my extensive reading of the classics, I put together an ad I felt sure would get Rieger's attention.

"Me worry?" Chuck Rieger: "Yes"

The headline, in the familiar format, read: "Me worry?" Then, a short, serious message followed: Rising costs plus the stringent buying practices of utilities have made it almost impossible for us to play the leading role expected of GE. The last paragraph, in response to the question in the headline, was a single word: "Yes." Rieger's bold signature "Chuck" plus formal name and title appeared below a picture of Alfred E. Neuman, the spokesman for *Mad* magazine.

Ingmire gulped hard, but sent it on to Rieger. Who promptly shot back: "Great! Run it in the next issue of *Electrical World*." This was the trade bible of the utility industry.

There have been a few account executives in this world who have protected creatives from burning at the stake. Fortunately, Ingmire was one of them. He tactfully suggested that we just plate the ad so Rieger could privately send reprints to selected customer friends. Which Rieger, reluctantly, agreed to do.

Anyone who has ever proposed an institutional communications program knows that it's difficult to prove how effective your efforts have been, let alone define what you hoped to do in the first place. A&SP did establish four clear goals with the "Whither" program in the antitrust aftermath: develop a vigorous new look of leadership; promote new ideas for industry growth; introduce GE's new management team; and pave the way for salesmen to promote products.

To see if any favorable mind-bending occurred, A&SP queried 99 utility executives a couple of years after the program had been launched. The response was encouraging: "A commendable willingness to undertake leadership and research." "It indicates GE is a progressive, alert company." ". . . GE recognizes the importance of maintaining leadership of free enterprise."

Many A&SPers, however, measured the program a success by the sight of Rieger happily escorting a utility president to the putting green of the Lake Placid Club at 2 a.m., during the 1962 Utility Executives Conference. "Turn on the lights!" roared Rieger. "Me and my friend are going to putt for a reactor!"

VIII
SHAPING
UP

❧

"Let me get this straight," said GE Chairman Fred Borch to Bruce Laumeister, who had just proposed that his Elec-Trak tractor business manufacture, and then promote through A&SP, a GE electric car. "We're already going head-to-head with IBM in computers, United Technologies in jet engines, DuPont in plastics, and Westinghouse in atomic power plants. You're saying," he added, through a smile stiffened by incredulity, "that you also want me to take on Ford and General Motors?"

In 1987, GE Senior Vice President of Corporate Relations Frank Doyle looked back at the 1960s and described the period of explosive growth as "falling uphill." In that context, he mused, "Maybe we didn't do all that much."

At the time, it seemed like a lot indeed.

Major new growth ventures

All at once, GE faced the challenge of getting its arms around what President Borch described as "the greatest array of major new growth ventures in its history." His response, in 1967: the first major company reorganization in 16 years. He doubled the number of groups, boosted the divisions from 29 to 46, and added 40 new product departments.

He also proclaimed earnings growth as a primary corporate goal.

For A&SP, this sharpened the dilemma that had dogged it for more than a decade: do you take on everything for everybody, as a loyal member of the club or, since your performance is still measured by P&L, do you concentrate on the more profitable market niches as the more likely strategy for survival?

A&SP knew at least what it did not want to do: become just another big communications agency. Many people in A&SP viewed those big guns on the outside in the context voiced by Curt Hockemeier: "15% commission and 85% bull."

A&SP takes aim

The time had come, General Manager Rallie Reid felt, to slow down and sort out the options – set goals, position A&SP vis-à-vis competition, perfect techniques, and get ready to take advantage of all those glory days that were supposed to lie dead ahead.

One key element of A&SP's mission quickly came into focus: long-term success would hinge on doing business with the "comers," those GE components which mirrored high growth segments of the economy.

A first step, then, was to identify which ones to go after. Borch had defined the major businesses in 1967: information systems, nuclear energy, advanced commercial aircraft engines, and new chemical products. An electric car, let alone the Elec-Trak tractor, did not make the list.

A&SP by this time had taken the measure of computers and atomic power and had pretty well settled on account strategies for them. But it decided to put on hold another promising futures business – jet engines.

GE jet engines: on hold

In order to break into the commercial market, GE had talked Convair into powering its new 880 and 990 jet transports with a GE engine developed for the military. It was great for the latter, where speed and power counted more than efficiency. But compared with the engine developed by Pratt & Whitney for the Boeing 707 and Douglas DC8, it was a turkey. It gulped fuel as if there were a leak in the wing tanks, advertising the flaw with a trail of black smoke wherever it went.

A&SP couldn't brag about much of anything until GE introduced the CF6 series in 1967. These highly efficient and reliable jet engines slowly turned the picture around over the next couple of decades until sales ballooned to $8 billion and GE's commercial market share soared to as high as 65% of the free world available. Then, promoting GE's position was easy. All one had to do was to follow the advice of the client who, outraged at the claims of competitors, told Bill Bernbach: "I've got a great gimmick. Let's tell the truth."

A crowd of A&SPers stood ready to see that the word got out. In addition to those on the account within A&SP, there were at various times ex-A&SPers Len Dalquest, Joe Reilly, Norrie Kenyon and John Caccese at the client's base in Lynn, Mass., while Jerry Perazzo and Greg Haas held forth at the jet engine plant in Evendale, Ohio. Doremus & Co. handled part of the business out of Boston, with the account team headed by ex-A&SPer Garrett Sheahan, twin brother of Gerry, of GE Corporate Marketing and Sales in Fairfield. Gary also put one of his staffers, ex-A&SPer Scott Vogel, on site in Evendale to keep an eye on everyday matters.

Plastics: too big to be ignored

The fourth major growth business identified by Borch was chemical products – i.e., plastics, along with such corollary lines as silicones, laminates and insulating materials.

A&SP had fanned the flame of interest at plastics a few times in the past, but almost always it quickly sputtered out. It flared brightly once during an A&SP pitch when the presenters wore jackets sporting embroidered monograms with the GE replaced by GC, for General Chemicals. This played to the feeling in plastics that while they might be a part of the company organizationally, they weren't going to act like the rest of the staid old firm, and didn't want to be lumped in with it either.

A&SP dutifully kept driving the 60 miles over the mountains between Schenectady and Pittsfield, knocking on doors to pick up pieces of collateral. Finally, things improved to the point where A&SP secured its first ad from plastics – in a program for the Olsonite Tennis Classic in which plastic buyers from the Big Three automakers were participating. Whoopee.

The business segment was so big and growing so fast that A&SP couldn't ignore it. To put this in perspective, it was GE and not some chemical company that came up with two of the three major inventions in engineering plastics – Lexan and Noryl. Also, GE actually sold more engineering plastics than DuPont or Celanese. And if that weren't enough, a young skyrocket named Jack Welch had energized the business, spurting in six short years from general manager of the Plastics Department to group executive of Components and Materials, two huge steps up.

A&SP concluded, reluctantly, that rather than take a further licking from plastics, it had better join them. So in 1976, it opened a Pittsfield office, with a full complement of account, creative and press relations services, under the direction of Office Manager Curt Hockemeier.

Fending with Ross Roy

Almost immediately, the move paid off. Plastics asked A&SP to put together a presentation for a visiting, top level customer – President Toyoda and his staff, from Toyota Motors. A&SP then sold a major Genal phenolics program, and for the first time – in competition with Ross Roy New York, the agency of record – snagged an ad campaign. This led to a major integrated program for Valox plastic. In early 1978, A&SP again won an advertising competition with Ross Roy, for Noryl products.

This increasing sophistication in plastics led A&SP that same year to propose a far broader integrated program to Chuck Carson, vice president and group executive of GE Engineered Materials. After the presentation, Carson called A&SP's Bob Ingmire, who headed the A&SP effort: "A&SP should make some acquisitions ... buy Ross Roy and shape them up. They can't match your ideas. You've got the whole order – *Wall Street Journal* program plus *Business Week* and trade program."

To show there were no hard feelings, the following year A&SP agreed to have its Pittsfield crew handle just the collateral for a new Plastics Division venture while the space was to be handled by... Ross Roy. Getting along with them was easy – Ross Roy's rep was ex-A&SPer Tom Keller, who now is vice president of corporate communications for Siemens.

These were the high-roller years in Pittsfield, with A&SPers – often in transition within GE from agency to client side of the business – churning out a huge volume of superb programs. A particularly significant one was dreamed up by ex-A&SPer Greg Bronk, a plastics ad manager tabbed by his top management in 1977 to help bail out a related business, GE capacitors.

Greatest juice since electricity

Capacitor products for many years had contained insulating fluid laced with PCBs which everyone – including govermental regulatory bodies – thought were great because the fluid was fire retardant and, therefore, safer than plain old oil. When people finally recognized the environmental hazards from PCBs, GE quickly devised a benign substitute. The challenge to Greg, along with Janis Mansfield of his own staff and A&SP's associate creative director in Pittsfield, Bob Whitney, was to let the world know that GE's new Dielektrol fluid was the greatest juice to come along since electricity.

The strategy, as you might expect, was to emphasize the positive. GE first kicked off its message at a press conference in New York City and a three day customer meeting at the Lake Placid Club in upstate New York. Then, it aimed a salvo of six mailings at end users, equipment manufacturers who used an insulating medium in their products, and influential governmental officials.

These were more than colorful fliers. Each was keyed to components contained in the mailings which the receiver could assemble in sequence to form a 10-gallon aquarium. The message for the aerator, "Living in Balance," explained how the device helped keep water pure to protect aquatic creatures – as did Dielektrol. "Light for the Living" was keyed to the function of the aquarium light, and so on.

Mailing four tons of gravel

A&SP's Schenectady warehouse handled the complex distribution of components, including four tons of gravel divvied up into mailing pouches. Wisely, the final program element – 30 tons of water – was not mailed. Instead, it became the door opener to executive suites across the country. GE capacitor salesmen hand-delivered plastic bags filled with water and, of course, exotic fish for the aquarium . . . along with a concluding plug for Dielektrol fluid.

This GE promotional thrust did far more than sell products. As Luke Hart, the general manager of capacitors later wrote to Bronk and Whitney: "Your contributions revolutionized our business and thinking."

With sales booming, A&SP added to its on-site Pittsfield staff and promptly picked up two more product accounts in competition with area agencies. But relationships began to deteriorate, more and more generating the heat of friction instead of the fire of creativity. By mutual consent of A&SP and client, the Pittsfield office closed in 1980.

A&SP continued to service the account from Albany for a couple of years, under the direction of Bill Hewlett. In spite of solid inroads, there was something basically wrong with the chemistry: Albany and Pittsfield just didn't mix very well.

Maybe it was the brash youngster thumbing his nose at the

dignified old gents from the world beyond the mountains. Maybe it was the resentment that festered in some ex-A&SPers in plastics for their former co-workers still on the agency side of the business. Whatever, account servicing again terminated, by mutual consent.

Borch had not listed electronics on his list of comers, but it was implicit in that context within a company with a name like General Electric. But Borch wasn't the only one to give it short shrift. Over the years, electronics was treated like a Westinghouse orphan at a GE family reunion. Alternately, people fawned over it and then rejected it, making it difficult for A&SP to position and promote the business.

Charting a future for electronics

Early on, GE had painted a promising future for electronics. It boasted in 1960 of "the two most important developments since the transistor" – the silicon controlled rectifier, or SCR, which stimulated a brand new department in Auburn, NY, and the tunnel diode, which cleared the way for ultra high speed computers. In 1960, electronics was included among the five sectors, the big operating building blocks of the company.

Yet the following year, it was not on the list of "major new growth ventures." A year later, Borch said there was no way GE could meet its long-term goals set in 1962-63 without "new ventures beyond the basic core of electrical and electronics."

The dichotomy continued. In 1970, GE introduced a broad new line of measurement, telemetering and process control systems – GEMAC, GETAC and GEPAC – which were heavily dependent on electronics. Concurrently, the organizational heart of the business was dropped a level, to division. A year later, GE sold its IC (integrated circuit) segment of the business, at the same time it disposed of vacuum cleaners. That in itself told you something.

The following year, in 1972, corporate visualized the company as a circle of related technologies. The business showed up only as a small segment labelled "Electronics and Home Entertainment Products." GE again omitted it from its list of "fast growing industries" a couple of years later. As if to underline that, it sold its GEPAC process computer business. This, it said, would allow GE "to concentrate more of its resources on automation systems for industrial and utility customers." To certain A&SPers, this was hard to accept, since they had been busily promoting

GEPAC computers for industrial and utility automation systems.

In 1976, electronics was not listed as one of GE's six historical business categories. But by 1980, with the ascension of Jack Welch, it was to be a "dominant technological force" to meet the "fundamental challenges of the '80s," mostly through microprocessor-based products. Underlying this resolve, GE put up a brand new microelectronics facility and an industrial electronics plant in North Carolina.

Help, of sorts, from RCA

In 1984, GE again appeared to be cranking up in semiconductors and ICs. Late the next year, GE bought an added stake in electronics through RCA for $6.3 billion. Shortly thereafter, GE said it got more than it wanted in the acquisition and would be interested in selling parts of its semiconductor business, which it later did.

For A&SP, then, the question was: how do you portray this pulsating, amorphous mass in a way that will make customers want to come to GE?

You look for star products, of course. But prior to RCA there weren't many and most of them were in a narrow band known as power devices – mosfets, optos, etc. On the other hand, general managers were happy if you just talked about commitment. The track record of the business, however, didn't give you much of a base to build on.

What you usually wound up trumpeting was GE's full line. This wasn't easy because the various electronic departments were free to do their own thing, and they generally didn't want to spend *their* money promoting somebody *else's* wares.

A&SP vs. Doyle Dane and BBDO

Occasionally, one of the departments would grab for the leash of leadership by coming up with a division program. At one time, three of them headed on a collision course – an A&SP-prepared program for the Power Electronics Semiconductor Department, one prepared by Doyle Dane for GE's Intersil unit, and a BBDO campaign authorized by a new division ad manager hired from the outside.

The latter prevailed and, while no big splash ever happened through a division space campaign, he did issue guidelines for ads and brochures produced by the individual departments. The key adhesive, he proclaimed, would be a common red color to be used in all work, and he admonished A&SP to monitor GE's output and keep an eye on competitive activity. Which led A&SP's account rep to call one day and report sadly: "Ron, someone else is using your color."

Activity didn't perk up much even with the acquisition of RCA, which in many ways outshone GE in electronics. Editorially, however, one heard a faint sound reminiscent of earlier days, when *Electronics* magazine reported in mid-1987 that GE was "returning to the commercial computing business" with a version of a high speed processor developed for the military. For computer veterans of both GE and RCA, it was as if an archaeologist, upon opening a sarcophagus in the pyramids, had been startled by a cricket which emerged to chirp weakly and then disappear.

Most GE growth businesses nestled firmly in the upper left segment of the four-block grid used to chart the future at business reviews. They were the Stars, to be nourished and encouraged. Others languished in the lower left as Harvest businesses, or stood stolidly aside for milking as Cash Cows.

Sometimes, A&SP found great opportunities in businesses that seemed to rattle around aimlessly from box to box. One of these was the heavy-duty, land-based gas turbine, an offshoot of GE's work in aircraft jet engines. Soon, some began to be used as prime movers in industry, driving pipeline compressors, for example. But the company's major interest was to build a new business using them as power generators, much like steam turbines.

Gas turbines and the hockey stick curve

A&SP account people sat in on a seemingly endless series of gas turbine business reviews where the recurring key visual aid was a Hockey Stick curve – business was projected flat for a couple of years, then it rose on a very steep, straight trajectory. Each year, the reviewing manager moved the stick a notch farther out, then waxed glowing about what would happen then.

During those early years, A&SP proposed to supplement a modest trade advertising schedule with a few full pages in *The Wall Street Journal.* There was the usual lament that this was a waste of money since the *Journal* reached three quarters of a million people and all that GE really needed to target was 100 utility executives. The refrain, of course, was that it was the only medium that would reach all 100, and you could also count on maybe the same number of influences upstairs in GE. As faithful readers, they were even more important.

In just a couple of weeks, a vice president of Commonwealth Edison called the GE district manager of utility sales in Chicago to say: "I just saw another one of your ads on gas turbines in *The Wall Street Journal.* If you're spending that kind of money on them, you must be serious. Come on over and let's talk." The salesman went, and the utility bought.

In spite of intensive advertising, gas turbine sales to utilities lagged. One deterrent was installation, which took place in stages as if it were a big, conventional steam station. GE decided to bundle everything up into a package plant which could be dropped into place quickly and easily. Sales still were sluggish, so the new head of gas turbines, Whit Ridgway, decided to cut lead time to practically nothing by manufacturing for off-the-shelf delivery. This was a huge gamble on his part because the packaged power plants, put into inventory, represented big bundles of "dead money" on the balance sheet.

1965 blackout: not all bad

The ill fortune of others brought good fortune to Whit. The catastrophic power blackout of 1965 prompted utilities to scramble for new power backups that could go on line quickly. A&SP's ads for Ridgway simply said, in effect: "We just happen to have what you need. In quantity."

Not that advertising was needed. Harry Carlson, the utility sales manager, said later that all he had to do was sit by the phone and take orders.

So gas turbines, once considered a receding futures business, became a widely accepted power source. GE went on to build and hold a commanding worldwide market share.

A small group of entrepreneurs, squirreled away in another part of the Schenectady Works, built on the early pioneering done by GE in the medical field. The X-Ray business, stemming from the invention of the X-Ray tube by GE scientist Coolidge, had just been renamed the Medical Systems Department, located in Milwaukee.

A&SP's Chicago office tracked the latter, while A&SP headquarters dropped in on the Schenectady contingent, chartered to exploit the exotic fringes of the market. Walt Robb, who would later head the GE corporate R&D center, directed the expeditions. Further impetus came from Jack Welch who, as head of the Chemical & Metallurgical Division, pushed for new uses of plastics in the medical field.

Initially, A&SP picked up a couple of promotional projects from the group in Schenectady. One featured the Peacemaker, a system of silicone earplugs that could be personally fitted to individuals. Another promoted the GE-Peirce Lung Oxygenator which purified the blood of patients with a porous membrane made of GE plastic.

Leonardo who?

A proposed A&SP brochure layout for the latter featured on the cover the famous spread-eagle drawing of a man by da Vinci. Bob Howsam, who made the presentation, came back shaking his head. "The engineer in charge said he liked the drawing a lot, but wanted to make sure we could find someone who could make the finished art do justice to the layout. I told him, 'Don't worry. I know just the guy.' "

Shortly thereafter, Robb took the business with him to Milwaukee when he left to head Medical Systems. A&SP tried but couldn't dislodge the agency of record, the Brady Company, which had a solid track record with the client.

In exploiting markets of opportunity, A&SP reached beyond traditional industrial media. In the process, it competed head-on with consumer agencies, and became moderately successful.

Consumer peak

A&SP's practice field, for starters, was the Louisville office, which opened in 1964 and, during the decade before, various segments of the major appliance arena. A&SP also expanded its consumer work into other areas of the company. In 1976 – probably the peak year – A&SP placed 28,000 radio spots generating an estimated 500 million gross impressions, produced five million newspaper tabloids, placed 6,000 GE ad pages and 15,000 Yellow Page listings reaching 50 million households.

From earlier days, the department had decided not to directly compete with Y&R and BBDO on GE consumer campaigns. So most A&SP Louisville output was for sales support coordinated with major appliance ad schedules – four-color newspaper inserts in the U.S. and Canada, in-stock point-of-purchase materials, dealer Trim kits, Use and Care manuals, mailings to specifying engineers throughout the world, A&SP-produced dealer and employee films, etc.

Central air conditioning opened its doors, if only a notch. It commissioned A&SP to place a two-month flight of TV spots, then prepare a half million dollar integrated program of TV, radio and print for target cities in the northern region. A&SP also worked jointly with Y&R to produce a trade package ranging from billboards and ad mat books to dealer information kits, decals, and T-shirts.

Industrial customers are consumers, too, so A&SP often used consumer media to promote business goods. Billboards and drive-time radio targeted automotive prospects for GE control in Detroit and Chicago, while TV spots generated traffic for the A&SP exhibit at the International Machine Tool Show. During the two years in which A&SP prepared radio spots for the Evansville, Indiana, Service Shop, the orders budget for the latter mushroomed 14 times while the facility grew from 600 to 3500 square feet. Said Evansville's Bill Weaver to A&SP's Dick Huether: "Many shop managers say they can't afford radio ads. I say they can't afford not to."

Stalking McCann, Chiat Day, etc.

Often, these excursions into unfamiliar territory gave A&SPers the chance to sharpen their competitive skills against world class contenders. In 1977, for example, A&SP went head to head with McCann-Erickson and snagged the $1 million consumer account for GE's battery business in Gainsville, Florida, spanning TV, radio, and print.

Such consumer capers were the exception rather than the rule. More often, A&SPers discovered agencies like Ross Roy sticking their noses under the GE tent. One would abruptly confront the beady eyes of Doremus or Rumrill-Hoyt in Lynn, Marsteller in Chicago, Doe-Anderson in Louisville, Ketchum in Philly, Chiat Day in Fairfield, and a host of others sniffing around the fringes. As often as not, the account rep or agency principal was an ex-A&SPer.

In those competitive frays, being inside the company gave A&SPers an unfair advantage for an unusual reason: outsiders usually didn't have the patience or the desire to wade through GE's bureaucratic molasses. Also, the irascible nature of some GE clients did more to ward off competing agencies than any strengths A&SP might have.

One of the most difficult clients was information services in Bethesda, Maryland. A&SP's Washington office turned out some superb work for them, but the component frustrated wave after wave of A&SPers – account people, special task forces sent on site, even one creative team I served on, headed by Bob Pulver, A&SP's general manager.

Della Femina to Bethesda: "Take a walk"

At one stage of mutual frustration, the client called in Della Femina, Travisano & Partners from New York City and began the usual stewing over a proposed campaign in *The Wall Street Journal.* One weekend, as later reported back to A&SP, Bethesda sent word to the agency to "get your tail down here right away to fix things." To which, according to one report, Della Femina told Bethesda in so many words: "Take a walk."

Bethesda patched things up with A&SP for a time after that, until it revived *The Wall Street Journal* campaign and insisted that A&SP place an ad with their headline: "We can save your assets." At which point A&SP took a walk, and we never looked back.

Actually, A&SP didn't have to go outside the company for competition. GE encouraged components with alternative products for the same market to have it out with each other in public. They often enlisted different offices of A&SP to lambaste each other's products promotionally.

Evendale, for example, suggested that heavy-duty GE gas turbines were wholly inappropriate for work on deep sea oil well drilling platforms, while the lighter jet engines they made were ideally suited. Schenectady immediately asked A&SP to create a 28-page brochure entitled "A Tale of Two Fillies" to set the record straight. This pointed out that a fragile race horse – i.e., the jet engine – was a pretty dumb choice for a job that called for a draft horse – i.e., the gas turbine.

In like fashion, the mechanical drive turbine people pooh-poohed the option of large GE motors for their type of applications, neglecting to mention that their own equipment was complicated and as big as a small house. Concurrently, the AC adjustable speed drive people and the DC motor people ballyhooed their causes to the same prospects, while the rapidly growing semiconductor business rejoiced in bad-mouthing obsolete electronic tubes. The latter GE business people just smirked and smiled, making sure that A&SP sent out their price increases. All the time, of course, they kept cranking out profitable spare parts, knowing full well that people who blew their old tubes couldn't replace them with transistors.

Going beyond "bash your brother"

Of course, A&SP had loftier goals than just "bash your brother." Along with sharpening the focus on markets and functions, A&SP honed in on incentives – actions that would make GE sales engineers more effective and GE products more attractive.

A&SP had been involved with countless motivational programs over the years. Product departments sponsored them as a device to get more sales time than other product departments served by the same pooled sales force. Because this distorted the leverage of different product operations, GE management began to tilt incentive program sponsorship toward the sales forces. The programs were particularly effective in revving up secondary distribution channels, where agents and distributors were the targets.

A&SPer Gerry Sheahan had a knack for this kind of work and, in recognition for producing many outstanding programs, he was hired by the distributor sales organization. He still leaned on A&SP for program support, and the fun and games proliferated. At least once a year, you could be sure to see in the corridors of sales offices and product departments giant posters showing GE participants dressed as World War I aviators, or gorillas, or cavemen, or whatever suited the current program theme. Except for the outlandish costumes, they poured forth the standard fare of company house organs – "grips and grins."

One could only describe the materials as a kind of cultural schlock, and top management chortled right along with the rookies. Ex-A&SPer Jack Peagler sent to Oscar Dunn, senior vice president of the corporate executive staff, a particularly grotesque poster showing GE's Erie motor management team decked out as Vikings. Dunn had formerly headed the department.

Erie bottoms out

Dunn was convinced that Erie had "bottomed out" with last year's poster, he said in 1972 in a letter to Jack, who was then the marketing communications manager. But, he added, "Consistent with the operating view of headquarters ('They never know what they are talking about') we were wrong!! It is our view that this will boost orders dramatically. Who wouldn't rather go out and sell than sit in the office and look at this picture."

When Sheahan's boss, Vice President Kris Christiansen, moved on to the Industrial Sales Division in the Fall of 1972, he brought Gerry along. He also commissioned Gerry to crank up an incentive program for ISD because the sales year was shaping up as a disaster.

This new group, however, wasn't made up of your usual distributor salesmen. ISD sales engineers didn't sell piddly components; they sold multi-million dollar systems. They also didn't sell to buyers; they sold to top execs. By reputation, they were staid, sophisticated, maybe even a bit stuffy. An incentive program for them? Kitsch, they told Kris. That's treating Tiffany as if it were a dime store.

To which Kris said: Baloney. I'm going to prove that you're as human as the rest of us. So he told Sheahan to figure out how to do it. So Gerry asked A&SP to figure out how to do it. The marching orders were explicit: this was Thursday, September 7, 1972. Gerry would be out of town until the next Tuesday. He wanted to review preliminary plans in Harrison, New York the following day, Wednesday, then present the program to Kris that Thursday or Friday. "I'll find the money somewhere," Gerry said. He wanted the program to kick off two weeks later, on October 1.

It was a fairly typical request for A&SP. And, actually, the launch date slipped only five days, mostly because of complex client approvals throughout the nationwide, 700-strong pooled sales force.

Christiansen was taking over from Vice President Wells Corbin, the long-time head of the Industrial Sales Division, which until the previous year had been A&SP's parent organization. Corbin wasn't retiring immediately, so the program had to recognize him, too.

Incentive sales: the 4th Quarter Stakes

Corbin, incidentally, lived near Saratoga Springs and favored race horses. The program, as noted, covered the year's last quarter. And everybody had a stake in its success. The theme, therefore, came quickly to mind: The ISD Fourth Quarter Stakes.

A&SP's plan called for each of the 10 sales regions to receive its own racing stable flag along with a registered set of jockey silks for display – Allegheny would get "BOF Brown," Eastern "Patchogue Pink," South Central "Pecos Purple," and so on. Sales districts were to take on the names of famous thoroughbreds – Citation, Twenty Grand, Whirlaway, etc. A huge silver racing trophy, the Corbin Cup, would be displayed by each monthly winner, then retired at the conclusion to its namesake, with smaller replicas staying permanently in the winning regions.

Individuals were to receive Winners Circle awards – specially designed jewelry, long stemmed roses for spouses, an inscribed silver Revere bowl to take home, etc. A&SP also proposed a Longshot award for extraordinary effort, the Sidesaddle Award for also-rans, and others. When results were totalled up at year end, grand prize winners from each region would be honored guests in New York City at the 21 Club – also known as the Jockey Club – where they would pick up their keys to brand new Ford Pintos.

30% VB equals $1 billion plus

Christiansen bought the program intact. His judgment proved on target, too. Even the most reserved ISD sales engineers pitched in to enjoy the fun. More important, industrial sales soared 30 per cent over budget, topping $1 billion for the first time ever. And, confirming the rule that governed any highly successful program produced by A&SP, Sheahan had no trouble scraping up the money to fund it.

Not all incentive programs had to do with sales. On occasion, GE manufacturing operations asked A&SP to help out with their problems, usually concerning productivity. Most of these never got cranked up to any meaningful speed because clients either wouldn't spend enough to make them work, or had preconceived notions that were awful. Or both.

Like Mobile Radio which wanted to launch something called "The Active Man's Extension" – A&SP told them they ought to go back and think that one through. Or the Instrument Department in West Lynn, which had already lettered up signs for their "Productivity In Sales and Service" program – we pointed out that GE people love acronyms, and would surely tarnish this one as the press did with the "Strategic Planning & Implementation Team" concept promoted by an area Chamber of Commerce.

Or Large Motor & Generator Department, which wouldn't budge from its proposed GOYA program, which stood for "Get Off Your Etc." – we declined. Or Apparatus Service, which was affronted when we said that HORSE was a terrible name for an incentive program in a drug-bedevilled society – mercifully, no one remembers now what the acronym was all about.

Sharpening incentive program skills may have been more fun, but most A&SPers concentrated on product promotion – looking for new and better ways to improve position, sales, and share. The form and direction of these explorations seemed endless.

Beetle Bailey, Car 54, punch-out airplanes

For the instrument products people, A&SP commissioned the comic strip's Beetle Bailey to underscore the "army of GE service people backing you up." Characters from the TV series "Car 54, Where Are You?" brought borrowed interest through print tie-ins and personal appearances at sales meetings. Someone in

A&SP conceived a VIP coloring book, which clarified a highly technical subject in a way that was enjoyable without being condescending.

For aerospace electronic systems, A&SP inserted a "punch out" paper airplane for an ad in the aviation books. Anyone who tried to fly it quickly got the point – it zoomed to the ground unless the GE radar cut-out was inserted in the nose.

One A&SPer came up with an exciting concept for a mailer – it unfolded on both sides, to a seemingly endless length. Production director Bill Berg, when asked for an estimate, reported back in two days that it would cost $7 million. "That includes the cost of a new press," said Bill placidly. "Nobody has one big enough to handle it."

A&SP program manager Frank Paul suggested a somewhat similar concept to introduce a radical new line of GE metalclad switchgear containing vacuum interrupters. "Put mirrors all around it," he said, "and we'll theme it 'Any way you look at it, we've got the best.' " Again, word came back from production that since the gear was pretty big to start with, the mirrors would have to be 50 feet long, 30 feet tall, would cost several hundred thousand dollars, and the special photographic effects would require a studio the size of a stadium.

The switchgear promotion and advertising that A&SP came up with was pretty exciting anyway, but the product department decided to slash the budget severely and rely on a product introduction built around a slick sales presentation. The reaction in the field was the reverse of the gas turbine advertising in *The Wall Street Journal.* One customer said, according to his GE sales contact: "That's a great pitch, but I don't believe you. If GE were behind it, they'd be advertising it for all it's worth."

A 72% direct mail response

An A&SP-produced series of mailers for DC motors was conventional, but highly successful. The product, one of GE's oldest, was portrayed as a Thoroughbred, a winning race horse with excellent blood lines that had been continually refined. Each mailer related to a fine reproduction of a recognized champion, such as Man-O'-War, and recipients were offered prints suitable for framing by calling their assigned sales representative. Seventy-two per cent responded, the highest total ever recorded for an A&SP mailing, and quite possibly a record for the industry.

The department also unleashed one of its distribution services experts, Shelly Wigler, to see what he could do in the esoteric world of deal-making. Acting as an agent for the consumer product departments, it didn't take Shelly long to place promotional give-aways on "The Price is Right," "Hollywood Squares," "The $25,000 Pyramid," and that all-time favorite, "The Gong Show."

Shelly could barter anything, it seemed. He swapped GE products for $100,000 worth of hotel room space for GE business use. He arranged a trade-off that involved a half million sweatshirts, which he ultimately sold off.

When the going got sticky, Shelly would sometimes bring along his boss' boss, Dave Jones, whom he referred to among his friends in the barter business as "my Show Christian." On one occasion, there seemed no way to budge Louisville, which refused to give A&SP a five per cent finder's fee for snagging a very large order for GE TV sets.

Shelly Wigler unloads toothbrush motors

Finally, the GE major appliance contact said he'd consider it if A&SP could help him unload a warehouse full of surplus electric toothbrush motors. "Give me 15 minutes," said Shelly, and he excused himself from Dave and the contact to use the phone.

He was back in ten. "You've got a deal," said Shelly, "as long as we get our finder's fee." He had sold the motors to Aurora, since they were perfect for slot cars. Shelly had learned the business well when he was ad manager for Lionel Trains before joining A&SP.

The increasing tempo of work produced by A&SP, particularly space advertising, whetted the interest of big-city media reps. *The Wall Street Journal* increasingly brought its big guns up to Schenectady including Don McDonald, who was just beginning his rise to vice chairman of Dow Jones. *LOOK* sent Gil Maurer, who later rose to become president of Hearst Magazine Divisions.

The old familiar faces from McGraw-Hill and Cahners showed up, too, but there were some newcomers. An eloquent spokesman named John Diebold arrived on scene to promote his book on automation; he coined the word in its present meaning. And the former science editor for *LIFE* magazine, Gerard Piel, unfolded his plan to turn a 101-year-old clunker he had bought called *Scientific American* into a respected medium for GE pronouncements.

The reps were solidly proving the old saw that the longest line between two points is a space salesman. That made it a princely time for A&SP's media manager, Ken Emery, who came to be called Sir Lunchalot.

The communications world was shaping up for A&SP, and for its people. The more A&SPers shaped up, the more they shipped out. Good men and women were hard to find and keep.

You get an indication of this from the roster for just one of the 40 subsections of A&SP during the 10 years beginning in 1962. The following is a partial list of those passing through Eastern Accounts (which never totalled more than 20 people) along with the last known destination for each after leaving A&SP.

Subsection roster: one of 40

Buford Barr, Director of Corporate Communications, Signetics, Sunnyvale, CA. Fritz Draeger, former nuclear PR spokesman for Pacific Gas & Electric, San Francisco, to Marketing and Hospitality Manager for Flora Springs Winery, St. Helena, CA. Peter Falcone, President of DDB Needham Worldwide, New York City. Ralph Goodwin, owner of an advertising specialty firm in Washington, DC. Carleton Hawthorne, deceased, one-time CEO of Wilson Haight & Welch, Hartford, CT. Steve Lyons, Regional Director of Ogilvy & Mather PR, Hong Kong. Jack Maranville, VP for Institutional Planning, Union College, Schenectady.

Dennis Maxwell, VP Corporate Marketing and Communications, SRI International, Menlo Park, CA. Doug McKinlay, of McKinlay & Partners (Motto: "Many fish bite when you got good bait") of Simsbury, CT. Bill Mick, VP, J. Walter Thompson, New York City, in transition to another agency. Jim Morey, creative free lancing in association with ex-A&SP A.D. Lou Gelinas, in Washington, DC. Bill Muir, CEO of Muir Cornelius Moore, New York City. Bob Muir, twin to Bill, CEO of Muir Associates in New York City. Dave Quincy, Executive VP of Colangelo, Greenwich, CT. Mike Rohan, an ad manager for Monsanto, St. Louis. Jack Trout, President, Trout & Ries, New York City. Paul Waring, head of an office design and construction firm in Atlanta. Bob Wells, Senior VP and Managing Director, Lord, Einstein, O'Neill & Partners, New York City.

Not counted since they're still with GE, but who worked side by side with those listed above, are: Jim Allen, head of plant communications and the "Voice of GE" for major appliances in Louisville. Steve Barber, manager of marketing communications for GE nuclear, San Jose, CA. Jim Harmon, manager of employee communications in corporate public relations, Fairfield.

Grady Hubbard, ad manager for GE Fanuc Automation, Charlottesville, VA. Dick Huether, head of GE Telemarketing, Albany. Jack Peagler, ad manager for DC Motors, recently retired. Jerry Perazzo, manager of communications for GE aircraft engines, Evendale, OH. Gerry Sheahan, manager of corporate marketing and sales-support, Fairfield.

All in all, things had shaped up so well that A&SP felt good about its position in GE. It was a major, profitable service department that contributed to the growth of new company businesses. It went far beyond conventional communications agency functions to provide skills and niceties that made life easier for product components. It was staffed, even stuffed, with highly competent professionals. And it was recognized and appreciated by top GE management.

In fact, many felt that things couldn't get much better. But not everybody.

The news bureau's Roger Hammond, for one, felt that a news release for GE's corporate R&D center stopped short of perfection. "There is evidence that the earth breathes," it proclaimed, "sporadically exhaling scattered puffs of gas at some places on its surface."

"Will we ever know," hypothesized Roger, "whether this constitutes a sign of contentment, a sigh of remorse, or some interplanetary hanky panky?"

Some people are never satisfied.

IX
ID
STUFF

"What do you think of our proposal?" one of A&SP's press relations managers asked Lou Wengert, a vice president of GE's computer business. "I think," replied the canny midwesterner as he arched his eyebrow at the flipchart, "you've got a bunch of feathers looking for a bird."

A&SP, with its charter to serve the entire company, was always one of the best places to view GE management in action, up close.

This was true at all levels, whether eyeing the lowliest sales manager or one of the corporate executive officers.

The higher the level, the more the managers shared common characteristics. One was a towering ego. Close behind was an enormous capacity for work. These were usually clues, too, that helped spot young Hot Dogs on their way up.

This isn't meant to say that all GE managers were overbearing, or martinets. Former Chairman Reg Jones, for example, was typical of so many gentlemen of the old GE school. Even so, he and all the rest knew what they wanted, right or wrong, and were determined to get it.

Recognizing all this made it easier to deal with them. And knowing that down deep they were human like the rest of us, made it easier to understand them.

It was also fun, if one didn't get too caught up in the spirit of things.

Pals.

When A&SP Manager Dave Jones retired in May 1987, he directed words of wisdom at friends and associates gathered for the occasion. To long term buddy and ex-A&SPer Gerry Sheahan, he aimed this volley: "The most important thing to remember in dealing with executives, is the difference between catering a party and being invited to it."

Gerry had already well learned the lesson of this gentle jibe, because over the years he had become expert in the care and stroking of GE executives. His skills were recognized to the point where one of his duties in Fairfield was to handle all of Jack Welch's management conferences.

Not everyone in A&SP recognized the difference described so clearly by Dave, and understood so well by Gerry. Speech writers, in particular, often teetered on the dividing line by hitching their fortunes to rising sons. When an executive went over the edge for whatever reason, the speechwriter would be left alone to discover, usually in utter disbelief, that he or she was neither loved nor indispensable.

Other A&SPers were drawn into a supporting role for executives, whether they liked it or not, simply because they were good at it. This included most district A&SP managers, who at one time blanketed all major U.S. cities to help prop up the company's varied field sales forces.

One of these was ex-A&SPer Ed Hicks, presently marketing communications manager for GE's turbine business in Schenectady. Ed was much in demand as a district A&SP manager because of his facility in handling meetings and executives. As a result, the one-time head of GE's utility sales division, Vice President Milton F. "Mink" Kent, regularly sought out Ed for presentation support, and to be a dinner guest at Kent's home, where he hosted many of the heads of corporate America.

A&SP's General Manager Rallie Reid took a liking to Hicks for an additional reason – they were both avid fishermen. So he recruited Ed to help plan and stage annual customer visits for salmon fishing on the Miramichi River in New Brunswick, Canada. It was fun, Ed observed, swapping yarns at the dinner table with guests such as famed Air Force General Jimmy Doolittle, invited by GE's host and boss of the jet engine business, Jack Parker. But Ed was always mindful that they were pals of the moment: the purpose of Miramichi was business and, as Ed knew well, his presence was corollary to relations – i.e., sales.

Even the guests came to realize that executive friendships are not forever. In succeeding years, more and more of the invitees retired and, therefore, wielded less influence in GE business transactions. Since genuine bonds of friendship had been forged, and since it would have been boorish to purge the lists, GE decided to drop the trips altogether.

Another A&SPer named Ed – Ed Sochor, who heads Sudden Impact, an audio visual firm in Westport, CT – balanced the executive support relationship in a way that was singularly successful. Almost everything he did was out of phase with regimental GE practices. Therefore, executives loved it – the more so the higher their level.

Ed was an art director on my staff in Albany for a time during the '70s. Every couple of months I'd get a plaintive plea over the phone from ex-A&SPer Bob Fegley in Fairfield: "Do you suppose you could spare Eddie for a few days to give us a hand?"

This was more than a mere request from Bob; it was actually a command. The "us" included Reg Jones as well as Fegley who, in his role as staff executive, wrote all of the chairman's speeches. Eddie, as visualizer, became the third member of the team.

Sochor had caught the fancy of the chairman for some past work, or maybe actions – he had a unique way with both. It very likely was at one of the GE management conferences in Belleair, Florida, attended by those at department general manager level and up.

Tempers flared during rehearsals at one of these as changes kept flowing in during the very early morning hours, with the conference scheduled to begin soon. Suddenly a shrill blast from a military whistle brought all eyes to the rear of the hall. Down the aisle marched Sochor, sporting a German helmet and goggles, to proclaim an armistice – there was to be no more sniping, and everyone was to go to bed. It perfectly brought the proceeding into perspective, and no one appreciated it more than Reg Jones.

While Ed's antics were well received upstairs, they often caused consternation in the basement. Answering another hurry-up call to join in on a Jones' talk, Ed clattered up to the gate of Fortress Fairfield at 4 a.m. in a battered Volkswagen bus, aimed his bearded face at the startled guard, and demanded entry.

When the guard rebuffed him, Ed crawled out of the window – the dented door had long since ceased working – and, as the General of the Guard and a bank of TV surveillance cameras closed in, loudly demanded a call to Fegley. The General withdrew warily, then reappeared in a few minutes with the word: "Let him in."

Sochor then proceeded to park his heap in Jones' reserved parking space. Hours later, another exasperated security guard finally caught up with him in the aerie of the rehearsal hall projection booth.

During the conference the following week, Jones spotted Eddie taking a break on a couch in the hotel lobby, seated next to A&SP's manager, Bob Pulver. "Hi, Eddie," smiled the chairman. Then, glancing quickly down at Pulver's nametag: "Nice to see you, Bob."

This was no reflection on Bob, since there were more than 500 other managers at the conference. Nor did it reflect any particularly close personal relationship with Ed. Instead, it was an expression of genuine appreciation by the chairman for Sochor's style, which sliced so cleanly through the bureaucratic jungle.

Prerogatives.

Position breeds power. Which, in turn, begets ego. Which often mutates in the strangest way.

For many years in Schenectady, GE's turbine business was a dominant force in the city as well as in the Works. It was therefore intimidating, and disheartening, to try and relax at the Mohawk Club, the town's pre-eminent social hangout. It was intimidating because one confronted GE management, representing a goodly part of the club membership. It was disheartening because the GE attendees always lined up before the bar in the rough order of the GE turbine organization chart.

Fairfield plotted prerogatives on a different scale. "You don't need an organization chart to tell how important someone is," averred Bill Berg, who was one of the last managers of A&SP's graphic services operation. "It's all in the recessed ceiling lights," he said.

"See that nine-holer?" he once pointed out to me. "That says you make $100,000. A vice president is good for a 12-holer. And so on up the line."

Out in the old line plants, the key to class was carpeting. The rule was simple, and everyone knew it: no manager's title, no carpeting. Once you made it, however, you could never be sure everyone knew it, because your office was usually behind one of the dozens of doors lining a converted factory hallway. So you advertised the great news through a simple device: on the planked floor outside the door, you tacked down a swatch of the same inside carpet. It nestled there vaingloriously until, over time, it took on a patina of grease and grime that matched the rest of the walkway.

Higher level managers were easy prey to prerogatives. When named to run new businesses, or to market new products or services, they invariably came on the run to A&SP after being seized with an uncontrollable urge: they wanted their very own name and logo.

I have at home a drawer full of tie clips, cigarette lighters, lapel pins, money clips, pens and pencils, pocket knives, measuring devices and the like. Each is emblazoned with a different symbol reflecting the impulse of a GE manager for a product, program, organization, or event. Most were produced in spite of two overwhelming arguments we always made against them: it takes years and millions of dollars to make a new symbol meaningful and productive, and the company already has one of the world's most meaningful and productive symbols, the GE monogram.

Most of these managers insisted on them anyway, along with another perk: their very own organization chart. They wanted one not only for use within the company, but externally, too, as a sales tool. And, of course, to sprinkle some credit on those who managed the venture.

In the '70s, we produced a six-page, four-color fold-out along with the usual logo at the request of GE's Manufacturing & Process Automation Division. This was headed at the time by Vice President Howard Kurt, who later left to become CEO of Hyatt Clark until it went under in 1988. The chart, printed and varnished on Kromekote, was gorgeous, with sparkling photos of individual managers as well as products and applications.

Kurt & Co. never used it for a couple of reasons. The first was predictable – by the time the piece rolled off the press, it was completely out of date because the organization had changed. The second was disastrous – a photo mistakenly supplied to A&SP by the division showed an impressive application, but the product was that of a competitor.

During the early 1970s, the vice president of GE's Industrial Drives Division, Robert C. Wilson, sought counselling from A&SP on – you guessed it, a slogan and logo. True to his reputation as a workaholic, he stretched the sessions into nights and weekends.

But the venture produced only design concepts and layouts, before Wilson left GE to make a name for himself by nursing back to health a couple of sick companies, Collins Radio of Rockwell International, and Memorex.

Oscar Dunn, who was vice president of GE's Transportation Systems Division during the '60s, understood well the allure of executive perquisites. To aid in his courting of railroad presidents, he came every year to A&SP for gifts that would be relished by this small, elite group.

One year it was a beautifully crafted captain's chair, with an attached brass nameplate serving as the place card at the annual presidents' dinner – and, of course, the chairs were shipped afterwards to each donee's home. Another year, it was a one-of-a-kind set of ceramic coasters, each tailored to the president's interest through – recognizing the universal urge again – his very own railroad logo.

One year, A&SP's Jerry Perazzo, who at the time headed servicing of the account, researched, wrote and produced an original book on "The History of American Railroading," complete with specially commissioned illustrations. On Dunn's strict instructions, only 50 copies were prepared, each leather-bound with slip cover, and specially inscribed for distribution solely to the invited presidents.

A railroad buff – like his peers, the most fanatic of all hobby fans – heard about it and sent Jerry a signed check with the amount left blank. Send me one of the books, he wrote, and fill in any figure you wish. No one could recall anything quite like it, except possibly another customer who came to a meeting in a sport coat which his wife had made from drapes inscribed with various railroad insignia. Again, the lure of the logo.

Dunn also understood the perks of power, and didn't hesitate to wield them when he felt they could influence business.

His marketing communications manager at the time, John McDermott, joined Dunn on a Friday to inspect the room reserved at the 21 Club in New York City for the railroad presidents' dinner the following Monday. Oscar took one look at the room, John related, and said: "Repaint it." The color, he felt, did not suit the mood he wanted for the occasion.

John's challenge was not unusual for a GE product department communications manager, except for one thing. It was New York City, and workers there liked to work only during the work week. If he could get it done at all, it would surely cost triple or quadruple the normal rate. John did, and it did. But when it was over, Oscar was serene in the conviction that he had catered well to the sensibilities of his good customers.

Ploys.

Recently, *Adweek* carried a column by advertising author Ed Buxton in which he observed: "There are many political ploys in agency meetings. Like when to arrive (late is better); where to sit (mid-table); when to talk (right after someone stupid); what to say (be noncommittal but a good summer-upper); when to leave (when your pre-arranged long distance call from a major client comes in)."

He could have been talking about A&SP. Or, for that matter, about the goings-on in the wide-screen GE world of management.

An A&SPer returned one day from a meeting at the senior vice presidential level. He translated what those attending meant when they said: "It's zero based" (it stinks). "Well, back to a blank sheet of paper" (we bombed out). "Let's stay flexible" (we can't make up our minds). "We'd better speed cautiously" (nobody knows what to do).

A&SP's Bob Ingmire also had to ask the vice president of the Apparatus Service Division, Pete Van Dyck, to clarify why he kept stopping and re-starting his ad program in the business management books when research showed it was reaching the targeted unknown influences. "It's my fiscal yo-yo," said Pete. "I let the program ride when business is good, but it's handy for quick money if it looks like I won't make budget." This wasn't the textbook answer Bob had hoped for, but the candor was refreshing.

Many people in GE also marvelled over the meteoric rise of Tom Vanderslice, who began as a brainy scientist in the General Engineering Laboratory in Schenectady, then went from section manager of an obscure GE business to sector executive in a few short years. Brilliance helped, of course, but he also got a boost from A&SP in his early breakout.

He had been assigned two minutes for a presentation in the Executive Office and, recognizing the crucial importance of the occasion, came to A&SP and said: "Make me look good."

The A&SP account rep recognized that it wasn't so much what was *in* the speech, as how it was handled. So he filled the two minutes with relatively innocuous material, but made sure that those attending would pose three questions, which were sure to stimulate discussion. They did, and the chairman, Fred Borch, became so intrigued with the ensuing banter that he invited the young manager to join him for lunch. The exhilarating ascent had begun.

A long-time GE business fixer from Canadian GE in Toronto, Carl A. Salmonsen, was a master at ploys which were transparent but highly effective. Top management sent him to various GE plant locations where costs had gotten out of hand, so he could work his therapeutic magic.

I caught up with him on an A&SP trip to Fitchburg, Massachusetts, where his first step had been to close the main entrance of the headquarters building and install the department's mail room in the lobby. "Nothing to it," he said. "Now, all the office workers have to enter through the factory, where they see the real work being done. That gets their attention fast, and guarantees cooperation on anything I choose to do."

Other management actions also were transparent, but not always so effective. "Bud" Beaudoin, ad manager for GE's atomic power business in San Jose, used to review the detailed printouts of phone bills in his staff meetings and, invariably, get steamed about the the high volume of expensive phone calls from Charlie Hamilton, his PR rep in Washington, D.C. During one of the meetings, in utter exasperation, he muttered: "I tell you, when I get out of here, I'm going to call him on the phone and chew him out."

Lou Wengert, the boss of GE's computer equipment business in 1967, saw A&SP's press relations proposal noted earlier as transparent, too. He suggested that the division program appeared to be a carbon copy of the PR program proposed separately to each of his operating departments. Redundancy, he complained. No sense of humor.

Management ploys, of course, could backfire. Wells Corbin, when overseeing the affairs of A&SP as vice president of the Industrial Sales Division, discovered this when he became disturbed that many of his headquarters sales people in Schenectady came ambling in to work from 15 minutes to three quarters of an hour late. No more, he mandated. Working hours are eight to five.

What he overlooked was that most of them stayed late every night and then lugged home a bulging briefcase of homework. When they got the word, they said: OK – shipshape at the office, shore leave at home. And they started to enjoy their evenings. In less than a week, the word was quietly passed to go back to the old system. Which in retrospect didn't seem so slovenly after all.

Another vice president of GE's industrial business, Bob Kurtz, also stimulated some unusual reactions as the result of his dictates. His background was manufacturing, and he was a stickler for order; he hated junk. He also loved plant tours. His idea of fun away from the office was to schedule tours during holidays or plant shutdowns as tag-alongs to his business trips.

When word of his impending arrival came, plant workers faced a common problem: most roosted in small cubicles with barely room for desk, chair and small filing cabinet. There was no place to hide things. Some solutions matched the best creative efforts of A&SP.

One group backed a truck to the loading dock and hauled away the excess, returning it when Kurtz left. Others took a different tack. Knowing the plant's mailing cycle, as well as Kurtz' itinerary, they boxed everything up and mailed it so it would be delivered after his visit ended.

Not all ploys occurred at high management levels. Some of those down low were so unreal, they seemed inspired.

For example, I once called a sector communicator to request copies of speeches that were to be delivered at an upcoming, high level customer seminar. The texts were to form the major content of a handout brochure to be produced by A&SP for the conference.

"The speeches are late," said the communicator. "Why don't you do a layout and send it out to stimulate some action in getting the speeches done. Then you can do your brochure." (How's that again?)

I then called the various product ad managers to speed things up by outlining for me what new material should be included in the speeches. The response from one: "Draft up some text for me, and then I'll give you my comments." (I don't know what I want, but I'll know it when I see it.)

Another time, I called a client to see why it was taking so long to approve a switchgear ad. "We've had 21 people OK it," he said. "We wanted to be sure." (He maybe should have asked Westinghouse.)

Planning.

Almost all successful managers at GE placed great stress on charting the future. The results were infinitely variable.

Stan Smith felt strongly that everyone in A&SP should have a Life Plan. He had committed his to paper when in college at DePauw, and began steaming along nicely toward his ultimate goal, CEO of the General Electric Company. He did pretty well, too, rising to senior vice president. But that wasn't good enough for Stan, and he left GE in 1973 to run the whole show as CEO of International Paper.

Stan left little to chance in his own lifetime planning. He had been known as John Smith in college. But that, he felt, wasn't distinctive enough for a promising business executive. So he sponsored a competition among his fraternity brothers to select a name that would strengthen his stature. And the winning name, which was all he was ever known by at GE, was J. Stanford Smith.

A&SP business plans were often tactical, reflecting strategic business plans of the product components. Few were more memorable than a "Long Range Promotion Plan" prepared by A&SP in 1958 for Chris Kastner, marketing manager of power transformers.

The 61-page document spelled out in infinite detail every element, action and cost that was anticipated for the five years through 1962. In short order, it went the way of organization charts – it became outdated, particularly when Kastner left to begin a steady rise to executive vice president and sector executive of the Technical Systems and Materials Sector in 1979.

This kind of planning was typical of much that stemmed from the Blue Books of the Cordiner era. Later, planning became much more sophisticated and "strategic," reaching an apex during the scholarly era of Reg Jones.

One of the first things that Jack Welch did when he became CEO was to downgrade and effectively wipe out the formal strategic planning process. As his director of planning, Michael A. Carpenter, said in 1985, "We don't need a lot of planners."

One reason for downplaying the planning process undoubtedly was the growing "someday over the rainbow" syndrome noted by GE's Senior Vice President Charles Reed in a talk to Elfuns. Leaning on Milton's "Lycidas," he warned that "The 'last infirmity of noble minds' is the mistaken view that the strategic plan is a selling document – instead of a tool to help the SBU cope with its real future."

At the same time, no one ever accused Jack Welch of not having a plan in mind and, even more pertinent, of not carrying out the plan. In a speech in Cincinnati in 1985, he observed: "It's not enough to complain about bloat and fat in the federal budget when we have it in our own budgets." At that time, of course, he was well on his way in gouging huge chunks out of the GE cost structure.

On occasion, planning could be a delight to behold. In sourcing a presentation brochure for top utility executives, I spent many sessions with the late Charlie Elston, one-time head of GE's large steam turbine business and later head of power generation business planning. I marvelled at the soaring concepts he envisioned.

Later, he chaired the board of trustees for the brand-new Schenectady County Community College and, one day, told me how he had solved a knotty problem at an early meeting. "Local boards tend to be political, as you know," he said. "They couldn't decide which bank to keep our account in. Finally, to break the deadlock, I said I'd evaluate them all and recommend the best.

"That noon, I walked up town to survey the scene. It was mid-January, and you know how the wind gets to you on Erie Boulevard. As soon as the first bank came into sight, I made my decision, and turned in out of the cold."

So much for sophisticated, long-range strategic planning by GE executive management.

Presence.

Management style varied immensely, and the prevailing climate tended to dictate the way A&SP conducted its own business.

The Cordiner era was buttoned-up and, therefore, everything A&SP did was by the books – by the Procedures Manual, that is, as noted.

Borch brought informality to the times, even though he was forceful as a leader. He constantly confounded A&SP AVCOM producers who tried to anticipate his needs at management conferences. To be safe, they'd always see that his talk was visualized with three-screen slides, like those of the other speakers. Then at rehearsal, Borch would invariably say to Doug Crossman, A&SP's manager of staging: "Dougie, don't use the slides. I don't want to have any disturbance. Just put the lights up for me, when it's my turn." And he rarely used them.

The smooth, suave Reg Jones brought grace and wit to the office, and statesmanship which was greatly admired throughout the business community. He laced his speeches with great turns-of-phrase. Some of the credit must surely go to ex-A&SPer Bob

Fegley who prepared the texts. But as Bob told A&SPers, the CEO "can write rings around most of us."

Jones, on prepping for the future: "There is no substitute for R&D and reinvestment, but, as a nation, we've been trying to do without it, and are now paying the price, like the farmer who had almost taught his horse to live on sawdust when the animal died."

On guiding the destiny of GE: "Moving General Electric is like trying to change the direction of a supertanker. It takes five miles to get one degree of change. But once you get it on course, you have to get out of the way or you get run down."

On GE's roots: "We are not merely 'a bundle of assets hastily thrown together in a feverish seach for profits,' as somebody once said about one of our competitors. Rather, we are a product of history, shaped and tempered by time. We have our legendary people, places and events – our Nela Parks and Association Islands, our Charlie Wilsons and Charlie Steinmetzes, our famous firsts and our famous failures. Out of all these and many other nameless, long-forgotten events we have forged a distinctive set of traditions, values and beliefs that we call the 'spirit of General Electric.' It inspires great loyalty, it encourages moral integrity, and it honors innovation. In my view it is one of our most valuable assets."

Other executives exhibited their own styles, usually reflecting their personalities. Jim Baker, sector executive for Industrial Products and Components, reinforced his outgoing image.

On automation, for example: "I think most of American industry has learned its lesson and knows that those who hunker down – or hibernate – during these tough times may never get up again . . . and that three choices face them in the eighties: automate, emigrate or evaporate."

And again, on why the Japanese government permitted an ultramodern factory to be built close to Mt. Fuji: "Pictures will show what is touted as the world's most advanced industrial plant with the symbol of Japan in the background. You don't have to work on Madison Avenue to get the message."

Vanderslice, who was a contemporary, maintained a much more dignified demeanor, somewhat akin to Jones. However, after leaving GE in 1979, he recognized that his business world was changing. He first assumed the presidency of GTE, and then moved on to become chairman of Apollo Computer. There, reported *The Wall Street Journal,* "the lordly Mr. Vanderslice startled workers by appearing on stage in a Luke Skywalker costume to do battle with a Darth Vader look-alike," representing rival Sun Microsystems.

Jack Welch's speech style is unique in a couple of ways.

First, he gets right down to business. In his initial speech to GE shareowners, three weeks after being named CEO in April 1981, Welch wasted no words. The first paragraph, in its entirety: "I have three subjects to cover in this 10-minute report."

Second, he's consistent. Later in the same talk, he described his vision for GE in a single paragraph: "We would like General Electric to be perceived as a unique, high-spirited, entrepreneurial enterprise . . . a company known around the world for its unmatched level of excellence. We want General Electric to be the most profitable highly diversified company on earth, with world quality leadership in every one of its product lines."

Everything he has said or done since then fits the mold: his three business circle concept, being #1 or #2 in every market, dual corporate citizenship (the resources of a big company, the agility of a small one), exploiting hi tech, crafting money machines, Work-Out, the software words for the '90s – speech, simplicity and self-confidence, etc.

Welch gets A+ for consistency, with one fortunate exception: he dumped the catch-phrase "Better than the best." It was not only bad grammar, it was an unreachable goal.

It was refreshing for A&SPers at GE to find that some of the best creative ideas came from engineers and scientists. For example, just one session with Jim Young, head of electric utility engineering during the early '60s, generated enough subjects and source to produce ads for the "Whither" program for three years.

The fertile mind of Guy Suits, who became director of corporate R&D when only 40, was a great idea source, too, from the '40s through the mid-'60s. He explained the process in a quote from the book "Your Creative Power" by Alex Osborn, the O of BBDO:

"It's generally a hunch that starts the inventor on his quest. Later on, perhaps after weeks of fruitless searching, another inspiration, arriving when he least expects it, drops the answer in his lap. I've seen this happen over and over. But I've yet to meet the coldly calculating man of science whom the novelists extol."

How stimulating it would have been to sit in on a brainstorm including Young and Suits, along with Werner Von Braun ("Research is what I'm doing when I don't know what I'm doing").

And maybe Iowa U's James Van Allen, discoverer of the radiation belt in space that bears his name. ("I have heard that talking to plants promotes their well-being and growth. I remain a bit skeptical. I talk to my apparatus quite frequently, sometimes soothingly and sometimes profanely. This may do something for me but my apparatus is altogether contemptuous of verbal communication.")

Sometimes, management made its presence known to A&SP in a – shall we say? – non-constructive way.

The general manager of a motor department sent to A&SP a sketch of the ad he wanted for his newest product – crammed call-outs, no copy block, no focus, but everything else except a picture of the factory, which might have been an improvement. "No changes," he dictated. After negotiations failed; A&SP politely told him to go elsewhere.

Then there was the marketing manager who insisted that the product photo on the cover of his brochure be straightened, to give it "order" (thereby ruining the graphic design). And the one who wanted to know what A&SP was going to put in all that blank white space in his brochure. To which his astute account rep replied: "We're going to fill it with dignity."

There was also the division general manager who insisted on blue for everything, because his wife liked blue. Or, the better reason given by Gerhard Neumann, who later detailed in his book "Herman the German" his life story culminating in running GE's jet engine business. He had been a refugee from Nazi Germany and, therefore, asked that A&SP not print things in red and black, the colors of Hitler's regime.

Personals.

Reg Jones was not the only CEO to steer a big, unwieldy ship. At a recent A&SP meeting, a consultant told of advising the chairman of one of the nation's largest banks on how to effect internal change. Regarding one action, the consultant said: "Why don't you just do it?" The chairman poignantly reflected Jones when he held up his wrists and said: "I'm in chains. For every six suggestions I send down the line, four of them just disappear."

Rank ambition: I was invited to accompany a group of six department general managers on a trip to Lynn to plan a division program on productivity. At the gathering in the hotel room that night, I was amazed to find that griping and sniping is universal, even though theirs concerned making their next jump, to vice president. The conclusion: "Close your eyes, and change the names, and it could have been a class of freshman trainees anywhere in the company."

❧

In Chapter III, it was reported that the 17 speech re-drafts for a UX conference speaker may have been a record for AVCOM. Wrong. Further research indicates that A&SP's art head, Walt Brzoza, visualized a speech for Oscar Dunn 21 times. When it was finally approved at a rehearsal in New York City, Walt was so happy that he had the script bronzed, and hung it from his drawing board for years.

❧

We sometimes forget those are real people we're talking to out there. To help sell a $30 million turbine to the board of directors of an electric cooperative in a small Texas town, A&SP produced a leather-bound, paste-in photo scrapbook that was personalized for each director. When the board attended a semi-business meeting at GE's pavilion in EPCOT Center near Disney World in Florida – even before the technical specs had been locked up – a lady director grabbed the mike from the GE spokesman and drawled: "These are nice people at GE. I think we ought to go ahead and buy their tur-byne."

❧

During a factory tour, a GE vice president innocently asked: "Why is that door painted green?" Nobody knew, so he moved on. An hour later, when he returned past the door, it had been painted Standard GE Gray, like everything else in the shop.

❧

An A&SP visualizer got a panic call to come to Fairfield the next day to do a speech for a senior vice president. "Be there at nine sharp," came the command, so he arose at 4:30 for the long drive down from Schenectady. Both the Veep and the sector comunications manager were huddled behind closed doors when he arrived; the latter appeared, sheepishly, at 9:45. Crisis: one of the $1500 fish in the Veep's office aquarium had died, and the Veep wanted to find out what was wrong. So he asked the communications manager to have an autopsy done; the latter returned at 6 p.m. to sit down with the visualizer and begin four hours of work on the speech. Said the A&SPer: "I finally understood what it meant to be a vendor."

❧

Jack Welch used to refer to himself as a "grunt." When viewed through his office window from a nearby wing, he does look like a good many of the other engineers scattered throughout the company – in shirt sleeves, head down at the desk, hard at work. But on his scale of doing, things are never incremental, but logarithmic.

❧

It is true that the formal planning process reached its apex under Reg Jones and its perihelion with Jack Welch. Yet written aspirations die hard. The preface of a 10-pg. GE product communications program proposal prepared in 1988 states: "This presentation focuses on the objectives of such a program and a plan for a plan."

❧

A&SP Program Manager Ray Roohan, telling a copywriter what he wanted in the copy for an ad: "Avoid clichés like the plague."

X

CROSS-CURRENTS

In an attempt to pull together its disparate offerings, A&SP in 1957 gave account managers responsibility for integrating what had heretofore been independent, functional services. I was one of those new account managers and, upon returning from my first trip to Erie, I dutifully reported to A&SP's handbook operation that the DC Motor & Generator Department's ad manager, Jack Peagler, had a justified complaint about an instruction book. To which Gil Smith, the long-time head of handbooks, retorted: "Why don't you mind your own business?"

In one respect, A&SP was a microcosm of the whole company: its highly charged components caromed like electrons around the nucleus of management. Often, it was as hard for the latter to bring the whole into focus as it was for clients.

Pressures had been broadly building for the company to get its act together. A&SP's Dave Jones recalls that, while helping Vice President Frank McCune get the Atomic Energy Commission to accept GE's position on nuclear liability, an AEC commissioner told Dave: "If one more GE light bulb burns out in this building, I'm going to throw your proposal on the trash heap!"

Business Week quoted GE Vice Chairman Ed Hood on a similar incident. At the end of a presentation to sell jet engines to an airframe manufacturer, the GE rep asked if the company could do anything further. "Well, now that you brought it up," replied the executive in charge, "I've got a problem with my GE

TV set, and my washing machine doesn't work too well, either." The GE man quickly phoned his service people to get the problem fixed.

But several months later, when asked if the appliances were giving any more trouble, the airframe manufacturer answered: "No. I've gotten rid of all my GE appliances." It was obvious, noted *Business Week,* that "each appliance stands as an example of GE quality, carrying a subliminal message to its owner who may well be a buyer of other GE equipment."

Issue: integrate or compete?

A&SP had never felt, over the years, any external pressure to integrate its operations. In fact, the company inferred that competition between units was good for total business. Sales figures tended to confirm this.

A&SP clients waffled on the issue. On the one hand, they welcomed help in preparing integrated programs that made them look good to management. At the same time, they suggested that A&SP people keep their distance. If you're front and center and do too good a job, someone might ask: "Who needs a marketing communications manager?"

So with the exception of Rally Reid's brief experiment in 1957 that set up an account section separate from the functional operations, A&SP pretty much stuck to its classic mold. The services went tootling off on their own, while the program and creative people lined up in copy/contact teams or in account groups supported by their own small creative pools. The groups, for as long as anyone could remember, were aligned by markets – industrial, transportation, defense, consumer, electronic, utility, etc.

In late 1971, the winds of change stirred speculation that a new course might be in store for A&SP as well as GE. Rallie Reid retired, after 17 years as A&SP's general manager, and shortly thereafter word came down that Reginald H. Jones would succeed Fred Borch as C.E.O.

Fred Borch and Rallie Reid move on

Most people in A&SP were unconcerned as to who Reid's successor might be. Promotion had always come from within, and any misgivings were always soothed by a familiar face; in a company as steeped in tradition as GE, there was no reason to expect otherwise. And, with 829 employees, including A&SP's Maqua printing plant, A&SP had a bursting reservoir of candidates who could, as Reid liked to put it, "stay the course."

The seasoned among GE management were not so sure, nor so relaxed. Chairman Borch had just outlined two goals for GE, heartily endorsed by chairman-elect Jones, that might change A&SP's comfortable way of doing business. This, in turn, might call for a different kind of leadership.

The two new goals: earnings growth, and social responsibility. There was nothing new in the first, of course. But the strategy to achieve the two together envisioned some distinctly new thrusts.

For two decades, GE components had gone their way within a sort of loose, corporate federation. Now, according to Borch and Jones, earnings growth was to be fostered by new GE organizations called Strategic Business Units, or SBUs. While still operating within a clearly defined orbit of related, or unified GE technologies, the new SBUs would transcend traditional organizational lines.

A new CEO goal: corporate synergy

Jones' early pronouncements made clear, too, that he hoped to achieve much greater corporate synergy. Toward that end, he served up a heady glop of corporate glue – plans for a new all-electric headquarters in Fairfield, Connecticut. This promised to funnel back levels of GE top brass, including operational heads, which had overflowed from GE's old headquarters in downtown New York City.

With such clear, corporate signals, then, the logical question posed by long-term A&SPers was: Why not a new general manager from corporate, to strengthen our ties? Certainly there were candidates aplenty among ex-A&SPers already there – Bob Fegley, for example, a staff executive for both Borch and Jones; Dave Burke, manager of all corporate communications; or Roy Stratton, the corporate ad manager.

The Sixties, at the same time, had sired a litter of young A&SP tigers who, growling in their lairs of discontent, disdained the conservative GE pace of progress. It was as if they sensed the coming of a new messiah as described by Kurt Vonnegut in his *Player Piano*. One could hope, of course, that they would be more successful than Vonnegut's arch-hero in trying to re-shape the Ilium Works, a thinly veiled reference to Schenectady.

In differing ways, all of the expectant A&SPers were right. Promotion for the new GM did come from within. But it was from within the company, not A&SP. For a brief period, too, the new GM did come out of corporate. On Reid's retirement, A&SP was reassigned from the Industrial Sales Division to Corporate Consulting Services. The vice president of the latter, Len Maier, toyed with the department by himself for a while. Then he installed as caretaker an acting general manager, Bill Cordier, who was quite content to be just that during the few months he was in office.

The activists get their wish

The young activists got their wish, too, when Maier appointed the real GM, as successor to the staid, conservative Rallie Reid. He was a 43-year-old, golden-tongued tiger named Wilford A. Lewis.

Lewis seemed to have anticipated the corporate call for social responsibility – he had recently run the government's Job Corps Center for GE, had been vice president of General Learning Corp., a GE joint venture with Time, Inc., and served as general manager of GE's Urban Systems Programs, which was gearing up to produce prefab houses. Earlier, he had helped in the development of GE guidance for the Polaris submarine weapon system, suggesting a competence in managing complex projects.

And, as he told A&SPers in his introductory talk, he was the son of a preacher.

The new general manager didn't look much like a preacher in his aviator glasses and Datsun 240-Z. Instead, Lewis appeared to be confidently striding along the line that divided the '60s generation from the Yuppies.

Will Lewis' four-point mission

His approach to things A&SP seemed more a response to the protest movement than to any measured message from corporate. In short order, he re-shaped A&SP in ways which brought badly needed modernization, but which went counter to its culture. These were sharply etched in four features: people, facilities, organization, and mission.

As one of his first moves, Lewis conversed individually with everyone in A&SP. He quickly sized up those who shared his vision, and those who did not. Just as quickly, he removed the latter.

In an overdue move, he warmed to the pressures from government to bring more women into the professional ranks of business. He appointed A&SP's first female section and subsection managers – the two levels below his own. Toward the same end, he inverted A&SP's traditional hiring practices. Whereas in the past one was surprised if the applicant ushered in for an interview was a woman instead of a man, during his tenure the exact opposite became true.

Today's accent, he avowed, was on youth. So for direct reports, he assembled young people of varied talents into a kind of palace coterie, which warmed to the task of focusing his vision.

New breeze: do your own thing

Lewis saw the conventional GE structured life as nothing more than a feudal system that stifled initiative and ideas. As a solution, he pumped life into the slogan of the '60s: do your own thing.

Up until now, no one in A&SP had been allowed to request people from someone else's operation without going through a complicated and formal chain of approvals. No more, said Lewis. Anybody is available to anyone, at any time. Not only that, he proclaimed, any person can go forth seeking a promotion without checking with his or her manager or, for that matter, even the personnel office. In fact, said Lewis, anybody could come to him directly about anything without checking the immediate manager.

As a kicker, he suggested that everyone in A&SP with any ambition should emulate his own career and, at minimum, change jobs every two years.

The consequences were predictable. With the exception of the remote branches, turnover of most A&SP groups skyrocketed. In my own 20-person creative/contact shop, it careened beyond 100 per cent before the first year was out.

As perhaps the ultimate product of "do your own thing," a fresh-out-of-college female art director in A&SP's Midwest branch produced an ad with no punctuation whatsoever. I wondered if she went overboard on reading the comment of *Des Moines Tribune* columnist Elizabeth Clarkson Zwart: "The older I grow, the less important the comma becomes. Let the reader catch his own breath."

Lewis then took aim at facilities. What had been acceptable to A&SP in earlier days – at least on a par with other GE operations in Schenectady – was by the early '70s drearily archaic. Proclaimed Lewis: if we're going to compete with outside agencies, we're going to look like one.

For starters, he established a standard, of sorts, in a re-do of

Reid's office. A&SP's art head, Walt Brzoza, working with AVCOM and exhibit specialists, transformed the somber old setting into a starship, with steering from a desk-side console that controlled video, lights, rear projection of film and slides, exhibits . . . every medium that A&SP employed.

In Lewis' game plan, however, the office was merely one dazzling jewel in a throw-away crown. The royal pull came from Connecticut, not Schenectady.

Down-sizing Schenectady A&SP

It would have been politically pushy to be at the front of the line of supplicants moving to the new GE headquarters in Fairfield, so Lewis devised a cautious strategy. Initially, he would extricate A&SP, to the extent possible, from the Schenectady Works. Longer range, he would aim for Connecticut. The client base in that area could justify being, if not at the foot of the throne, at least comfortably close on the dais.

As an expedient first step, Lewis in 1973 boldly lifted out of Schenectady his largest A&SP operation headed by Bob Ingmire, and plunked it into a brand new building on Wolf Road in nearby Colonie, Albany's suburban business hub.

Lewis was lucky. Many GE operations had longed to relocate outside the plant, but were told to stay put because it would upset the unions, the local city fathers or, even worse, the status quo. When Lewis made his request, business at the plant happened to be booming. So when the launch window fluttered open ever so briefly, he pressed the button. It was the beginning of the end for A&SP in Schenectady.

By the end of his first year, Lewis had removed a major portion of A&SP from its long-term bastion. He shifted his headquarters and staff, along with chunks of the advertising operations, AVCOM and the news bureau, to Stamford. Certain branches had been relocated and upgraded – the Chicago office to Oak Brook; Winston-Salem to Vienna, Virginia, near Washington, D.C.; and the San Jose office to suburban Campbell. Lewis even agreed in 1973 to open an outpost in Erie to accommodate the uneven fortunes of GE's transportation business. It quickly folded due to a mutual lack of interest.

Lewis saw to it that for the first time A&SP people – including those still at the Schenectady Works – had widespread access to the tools and settings of modern business: computers, word processing, open-area acoustical panelling, even potted plants and a choice of art decor.

The "new" Procedures Manual

Lewis also made sure that A&SP people got the word that things were done differently now. His staff published a brand new "How To" book, successor to the old Procedures Manual. The latter taught you to do everything but scratch, and that wouldn't have been unexpected. The old manual told you all about customer approvals, and competitive references, and use of the monogram, and the Robinson-Patman Act, and on and on. It even guided you in reproducing stamps and coins and in dealing with the Girl Scouts as well as the President of the United States.

The old binder really remained the "How To" manual; the new one grappled more with the "What" and the "Why." The revision of "How to Prepare Space Advertising," for example, skipped such things as the Need for a Policy, Responsibility, Authority, Mechanical Steps, etc. and concentrated on basic concepts and philosophy. In the process, it boiled down 87 pages to 11. It was great if, as a newcomer, you wanted to be on your own. If you wanted someone to hold your hand as you wandered through the maze, you were out of luck.

Lewis was one of the first in the industry to buy computerized graphics systems, adapted by a GE component in Syracuse from its work on flight simulators for the government. He had one loaded on a specially-outfitted trailer, and then routed it throughout the company. It graphically underlined to clients that A&SP was truly refreshing its musty image.

"You need how many slides by when?"

In the process, A&SP took on the equipment maker as a client, promoting GE Genigraphics slide-making service both inside and outside the company. One classic ad showed an art director leaning toward the reader, with doleful eyes absorbing the unspeakable but not unexpected request: "You need how many slides by *when?*" Copy then developed the Genigraphics theme: "It changes the whole picture."

The physical moves soon paled in the light of organizational changes. First rule, Lewis proclaimed: no more boxes. It was all right to use solid or dotted lines to show how A&SP people relate to one another. But, he said, never *never* draw an organizational chart with boxes.

Serving SBUs via the matrix

The reason, Lewis explained, was that A&SP was about to shift from the traditional line form of operations to that of the matrix, broadly used by GE businesses working with the military. This was the only way, he felt, that A&SP could serve SBUs, and not just the operating components.

This meant that A&SP would now field a new category of A&SP program managers – a giant step up from the old system of account supervisors – who were to be responsible for all dealings with clients, along with everything produced by A&SP.

Shades of Rallie Reid.

At the same time the program managers, true to the matrix mold, would have only dotted-line authority in integrating A&SP supporting services, since performance of the latter would still be individually measured. The charter of the programs managers, in other words, was to persuade rather than command.

Shades of Ralph Cordiner and the Blue Books.

Program managers gain clout

It soon became clear that these new A&SP program managers held stronger sway than one might expect. First, since they were to be measured on total financial results for their assigned accounts, they were given considerable clout in pricing. And second, since everyone knew they carried Lewis' strong backing, their words smacked more of commanding than cajoling.

A trace of the old market orientation remained in the industrial and utility operations, which stayed as flagships of the businesses in Schenectady and Albany. Other new ones adopted allegiance by area – Midwest, Atlantic, and Connecticut – or by function (the amalgam of supporting services was now called Resources) and by two tempting come-ons, Corporate and Consumer.

In regard to the latter, Lewis acknowledged that A&SP was not about to compete head-on with the BBDOs and Y&Rs of the GE advertising world. But he also was not about to ignore what those agencies had disdained – collateral business dribbling out from the several hundred millions in GE consumer billings, a chunk far bigger than the rest of the company's ad expenditures combined.

With everything at the ready, Lewis next recast A&SP's mission. This profoundly affected the department's future, during both Lewis' tenure and that of his protégé and successor, Bob Pulver.

With A&SP ensconced in corporate, Lewis convinced his superiors that A&SP should no longer be measured by P&L, like an ordinary line operation, but by cost recovery. This didn't transform A&SP overnight into corporate staff, but it bordered on it.

P&L bogey: from 8% to zero

Under P&L, A&SP typically had a net profit bogey of six to eight per cent. Now, it settled in at zero, plus or minus two per cent. Anything outside that became a problem. If A&SP relied upon advertising and sales promotion alone, that would indeed be a problem because volume was unpredictable; it was not unusual for December billing to soar to one fifth of the year's total. In 1980, for example, the volume for one week during that month ballooned to an annual rate of $395.8 million in billings, not capitalized.

A&SP devised a simple method to stay within its cost recovery range. Leverage came from the old back office business that agencies typically look down their noses at: the Mail Room. To A&SP, it was a huge financial sponge with which it could sop up or squeeze out money at will.

A&SP called its mail room Distribution Services. The unit stored and mailed millions of dollars worth of publications, customer gifts and incentives, employee awards, and company stationery. Since it had a captive market with predictable demand, A&SP adjusted prices to build up a hefty surplus by year-end. Then, to close the books, it simply bought enough supplies for the warehouse to bring the department's net in on target. A neat balance: operational flexibility, and corporate purity. Sort of.

Headaches from headcount

Even so, A&SP came under cost pressures like everyone else at corporate, primarily for headcount. This was nothing new, because all components went through frequent belt tightening, usually to cope with recessions. Then, the word would come down to pare back five or 10 per cent or whatever, across the board.

The last cut of this kind came when A&SP was glaringly top-heavy in 1969, forcing a layoff of 90 people. Interestingly, all but two A&SPers had jobs lined up before they left the payroll.

When Lewis first arrived, he proclaimed that A&SP was "adding capacity in a number of areas, including media, measurement and research and photography." The headcount, however, peaked at 565 and, perfect record on cost recovery or not, something had to give.

A&SP's high-visibility production operations went first – the typing bureau, the construction shop in exhibits, and the photo house. A&SP precipitated a near-disaster with the latter. It contained company archives of some 800,000 pictures and more than a million negatives, all scheduled to be dumped. Fortunately, GE's Elfun Society organized a last minute rescue operation, providing a home in its Hall of History, headed by ex-A&SPer George Robertson.

Not many A&SPers worried about further cutbacks. A management report stated: "As our work becomes more professional, there may be other kinds of work we shouldn't do, too. Christmas cards come quickly to mind."

The department's primary new mission, according to Lewis, was "to improve the productivity of salesmen." Henceforth, A&SPO (the "O" was tacked on for "Operations") would represent not only the organizational name, but Lewis' articulated goal: the Aggressive & Systematic Production of Orders.

A new three-pronged strategy

His strategy encompassed three thrusts.

The first called for the troops to offer traditional, functional A&SP services – slightly snubbed in, but still the most extensive line-up of communications functions available anywhere.

The second brought into play the program managers, who were to sharpen their consultant skills and take the lead in preparing integrated programs. These were targeted for the more sophisticated departments, higher level components and, of course, the free-floating SBUs.

The third thrust aimed straight up. A&SP intended to get in on more of the action at corporate.

In terms of the first thrust, then, it was business as usual for the cherry pickers. They could choose their ingredients from A&SP's long shopping list, and then serve up their communications pie as they saw fit, unadorned or à la mode.

Most components, however, were anxious to take advantage of A&SP's second offering – the preparation and launching of integrated communications programs. This invariably meant consulting at higher organizational levels, so Lewis saw to it that program managers got some sophisticated new tools that talked the language of middle and higher GE management.

Sales Task Analysis: justifying ad budgets

One was an analytical process called Sales Task Analysis. This showed clients how to separate personal contacts by their salesmen from non-personal contacts made through advertising and sales promotion, and then to see how each could be budgeted more efficiently. Ultimately, A&SP program managers demonstrated the process in client offices with hand-held programmable calculators, counselling with more than 20 of A&SP's 50 full service clients.

The process called for answers to 25 questions about the market environment and marketing effort for a product. The program then reported the balance of relative price, market share and spending appropriate to the product. Different models were aligned to various markets – capital goods, materials, components, and consumer durables.

By adjusting input, clients then could estimate how a change in market conditions and marketing effort would affect share, pricing, or spending of promotional dollars. This bolstered marketing communications managers, who now had hard numbers to support budget recommendations. A&SP pegged the accuracy of these market share predictions at 90%.

One of the first requests for a major integrated program came from an unexpected source – A&SP's former general manager, Stan Smith.

Smith had maintained relations with A&SP, largely indirect, during his climb through the company as head of Outdoor Lighting, Corporate Marketing & Public Affairs, GE Computers, and then International. In 1971, he had been named senior vice president of the Corporate Administrative Staff, one step below the Corporate Executive Office.

From Smith to Lewis to Burnside

A good many GE people believed that Smith had been the force behind Lewis' appointment as Reid's successor to head A&SP. This was never confirmed, but in this case Smith did tap Lewis directly to respond to a request from Peter Van Dyck, vice president of Apparatus Service. Lewis, in turn, asked me to put together a program.

His note read: "At Van Dyck's request, we will produce an aggressive sales promotion program (within three weeks) which will increase sales, reduce the time required for each new shop to become profitable by concentrated efforts with each shop opening, provide a basis (opening) for conversations with upper management in customer organizations, increase motivation and competitive spirit of service shop personnel, link sale of prime equipment when appropriate (and get excuse to see top officers). And, make John Blake, the marketing manager, and Pete Van Dyck rich and famous." The latter had been the motivational rallying cry of Smith when he was head of A&SP.

Lewis added this P.S.: "And, consequently, make Jim Burnside rich and famous. Will."

The challenge was typically Smith: stretch far beyond the normal scope of A&SP; link the leverage to business, not just promotion; tidy up the intricate relationships between the varied GE interests; then focus everything on a single theme that is meaningful to customers.

This was a tall order. The "varied GE interests" included six major business segments, with a host of subsegments; nine major markets; six geographical regions with 250 shops around the world; repair service for anybody's equipment, not just that made by GE; and 10,000 competitors, not including the captive shops of other big manufacturers.

Lewis and I delivered the proposal on time to Pete and his staff. Like most A&SP integrated programs, it was long-range, extensive, and expensive. After much deliberation, Van Dyck and his people decided the focal offering – GE Strategic Maintenance Service – would create too many turf battles within customer organizations, so the program was never fully implemented.

A year later, Van Dyck concluded that if he were going to do anything, it ought to be in partnership with his vice presidential counterpart, C. C. "Tip" Thomas, who had service engineers scattered around the globe – together, they could field a service army of 7,500 people. So A&SP mounted an extensive joint program, including ads in *Business Week* and *The Wall Street Journal* and an internal program promoting tie-ins from 60 GE product departments.

Anything . . . anytime . . . anywhere

Case histories elaborated on the theme "GE Service Is . . ." with the sign-off stating simply "Anytime . . . anywhere." A lawyer, typically, cautioned that GE should never make such a positive claim. Van Dyck, in a triumph for realism, responded: "Don't be coy. We'll do anything anybody wants, as long as they pay for it."

In one of the ads, the client wanted to picture the depth of experience in the Chicago shop and, inferentially, show that GE did not discriminate in hiring. So A&SP's Sal Cascio, who was art-directing the photo shoot, dutifully rounded up all the ethnic types in the place. The final print showed people from China, Korea, Pakistan, Mexico, and a sprinkling of blacks and whites who could have come from anywhere. It was a magnificent photograph – but the lawyer this time did manage to kill the shot: "Real or not," he said, "it looks too contrived."

This service program focused on customer recognition and acceptance, unlike the earlier one prompted by Smith, which keyed on sales results. So for second prize, A&SP had to be satisfied that nearly every spread in *Business Week* rated first in book, according to Starch readership surveys.

The integrated programs for Van Dyck brought together common GE interests in search of a common market. Just as often, A&SP focused the disparate interests of GE product departments with a common marketing objective. Major trade shows were ideal vehicles – the Society of Automotive Engineers, the International Machine Tool Show, and so on. For the latter, one of the largest, A&SP typically would integrate four sectors, 15 product components and eight sales forces.

Integrating GE advertising for a common purpose was harder. But in the mid-'70s, a survey of the contractor market showed that it was no less needed, and the climate was ripe. Eighty-five per cent of industrial end-user customers saw no difference between GE and other suppliers. One probable reason was that GE ad volume had declined 86% for GE's contractor equipment division and 48% for the company. At the same time, advertising by the industry as a whole had dropped by a third.

For contractors: "more than meets the eye"

A&SP teamed up with key GE product and sales people to mount a massive advertising attack. Theme of the program was "There's more than meets the eye" in the technology inherent in the 800 industrial product lines made by GE.

Each ad implied a benefit through a headlined query about the GE product: "What makes GE plugs, receptacles outlast others?" Answer: "Molecular Muscle" (a virtually unbreakable plastic housing). Or, "What tools are needed to inspect GE motor starters?" "Just these" (a pair of hands). Or, "What makes GE Gator Grip plugs grab so tightly?" "Jaws" (close-up of the clamping end, in a fair imitation of the poster promoting a currently popular movie).

Product departments paid for their own messages, but A&SP coordinated them as to format, scheduling and creative. Sponsorship, which initially came from 10 departments, three divisions and two groups, ultimately spread across half the company.

Two key measurements eclipsed any concern about readership scores. The program became a major element in the 1977 strategic plan of the Contractor Equipment Division's program to "Expand Core Business Market Penetration." And, from upstairs came the word: "Admittedly, I'm no expert, but these look good to me." Signed, R. Jones, Chairman.

BBDO "for the long run"

A couple of years later, the Industrial Products and Components Group – two layers up from the contractor division – tried the same thing, without much luck. Actually, it had better odds at start-up: the proposal was fueled from sector both by money and by an interest in automation, a priority company target. And to put the sizzle in its stake, the sector brought in BBDO, the corporate agency. Its job was to target top management; A&SP, to secure tie-ins with served product departments.

BBDO rolled out its big guns, from Research to Rosenshine, and unveiled the prototype campaign before assembled A&SPers and product ad managers. All the elements – ads, packaging, exhibits, P.O.P. and PR – keyed on the theme: "GE for the long run."

The rationale made a great deal of sense – "GE is a reliable company you can count on; we'll be doing the same thing whenever you need us down the road; etc." But what BBDO and the sector didn't count on was the beginning of the Welch era. Stability did not match the new chairman's view of GE's future. In a half-hearted manner, the sector decided to kick off the program anyway, sans theme, and quickly found that, in the short run, A&SP interest in format faded as quickly as the chairman's enthusiasm for the theme. Things soon settled back to normal.

The company, along with A&SP, probably integrated more effectively through periodicals than any other medium. As the '80s got under way, corporate could send out The Word via 600 different GE periodicals, with readership ranging from 25 for remote office newsletters to 30,000 for major plant newspapers.

Building a publishing business

A&SP published the bulk of the glossy external magazines, so it could report in 1977: "We're a respectable publishing firm in our own right. This year, we will prepare more than 120 issues of 12 periodicals, totalling over 775 pages, and reaching about

56,000 receivers (for a total of 275,000 copies), both inside and outside the company. One of these – you're reading it now – is a freebie." This referred to *Monday Morning,* the A&SP weekly news sheet prompted by Lewis to help keep his people posted on what the scattered A&SP offices were up to.

Over the years, A&SP churned out a huge number of periodicals, whose fortunes varied with the times: *The Sales Promoter* (for apparatus sales); *Welding Arcs; Trade Winds* (marine); *Electric Forum* (utilities); *Power Electronics; Impact* (telecommunications); *At Your Service;* etc. Dean of them all was *Industrial Power Systems,* known as *IPS,* a slick four-color piece that almost made it to age 30 before GE knocked the props out from under its founder and godfather, Don Brereton, along with the last of its many editors, A&SP's Don Wilcock.

Shortly before its demise, Don proudly reported to me and to the book's editorial council that the 25th anniversary edition was "the fourth consecutive edition to be released on schedule." This sounds ridiculous, but actually reinforced a creditable record: the book was financed on a tin cup basis for more than a quarter of a century by dozens of product department ad managers, all of whom retained approval authority. The fact that the two principals got it out at all, let alone occasionally on time, was a monumental achievement.

Aiming for the top

The first two thrusts in support of Lewis' mission – dishing up all kinds of communication services for GE, and then offering to integrate them – weren't all that different from what A&SP had already been doing. And the third thrust – doing more work for corporate – was not really new either. Actually, it could be measured better by degree than by territory.

For A&SP had long done work of a corporate nature. Sometimes it was by instinct, because GE needed it. Often it was by default, since nobody else had any interest in doing it. While many of these were mundane, they were highly effective.

For example, A&SP offered for a small fee to assure clients that their product listings in industry catalogs such as *Sweet's* and the *Thomas Register* would include a bold GE monogram plus a reference to the proper sales force – often a sticky question both internally and externally. Along with it, A&SP maintained a "Blood Bank" whereby distributors and agents could pick and choose from standard copy/photo modules and get from A&SP a tailor-made GE catalog. The department also published and sold a directory of GE Products and Services to product departments and the sales forces. As of 1979, the document was the only ready reference for some 3500 GE items covering 2900 categories.

A&SP backed into the role of supplier of company service awards – the jewelry and plaques that marked years of employment. These were a logical follow-on to the symbols of recognition and reward that A&SP produced over the years for promotional support programs.

Pass-along statistics

Recipients held both kinds in high esteem. A GE distributor salesman, on his death bed, made his wife promise to pin on the lapel of his burial suit his A&SP-created Master Salesman pin for outstanding performance. And, carrying the tradition one step farther, the gravestone of Donald Veeder in Evergreen Cemetery outside of Fonda, NY, proudly displays a GE monogram along with other vital statistics.

Corporate naturally turned to A&SP, then, for the trappings of company-wide cost reduction programs. These were predictable. Inexorably, they enveloped the company every four or five years – Operation Upturn in 1958, Accent on Value in 1963, Go For Improvement in 1967, Best Buy in 1971, ad infinitum, ad nauseam. One gained mild comfort in noting that the themes of other big companies rarely peaked on a higher creative plane – i.e., General Motors' multi-million dollar comeback program for 1988 was dubbed "GM Teamwork & Technology – for Today & Tomorrow."

A&SP reached the apogee of incentive sales volume in 1978 when GE marked its 100th birthday. During the first two months of the year-long celebration, A&SP shipped 400,000 items ranging from stickers to pewter plates.

The ease with which A&SP handled these large-scale projects led to other corporate-type work: distributing personalized benefit statements to all employees; distributing, then also creating the yearly GE calendar with a run of 750,000; preparing and distributing a million and a half GE diaries and pocket planners every year; and setting up a graphic services unit in the heart of Fairfield to handle top-level, often proprietary presentations.

While these were important and profitable, they didn't exactly add up to a featured role on the corporate stage. Furthermore, it was unlikely that A&SP would ever land one. Corporate advertising and PR, in concert with BBDO, usually skimmed off the cream of institutional programs and then, for collateral, called in A&SP when continuing contact with operating components was critical.

"Who Cares?"

This had happened in 1964, when GE initiated a program with the theme "Who cares if (fill in the blank)?" The answer, of course, was that "GE cares, and here's what we're doing about it (re: national defense, social concerns, the environment, etc.)." Corporate kept the TV and consumer media parts, and asked A&SP to put together a long list of ads for the trades. It may not have been the engineer's seat in the locomotive, but it was good for a nice ride in coach.

As a consolation, A&SP became the agency of record during the Lewis/Pulver era for such corporate components as GE Realty, Corporate Audit, and Corporate Telecommunications. As one indication of the business complexity of the latter, in June 1981 it received from AT&T a $7 million partial service bill that weighed 182 pounds, stood six feet high, contained 1,182 pages, and cost $152 to mail.

The challenge of complexity often made A&SP a sole supplier. For many years, the department produced the Chart of the Nuclides, a job its sponsors claimed no one else would tackle, and which they described as "The one thing GE produces that confirms we're the most technologically advanced company in the world." Some of the hyperbole probably rubbed off from the specs for the 50,000 copies of the 29″ by 49″ poster. To pull it off, A&SP required 10 different color combinations and 32 pieces of base art with the equivalent of 250 overlays.

A limited edition for Reg Jones and Elfun

Even GE's past was complex. When the Elfun Society approached its fiftieth anniversary, GE Chairman Jones noted, "We've been so busy making history that we haven't taken time to record it." As one antidote, A&SP researched and produced a 112-page book, commissioned by the turbine business, called *Reflections*. It described the early growth of GE through the eyes of surviving pioneers. The limited edition met the standards of most book collectors: original text, commissioned illustrations, end papers specially printed in gold, slip case, the 1200 copies individually numbered by hand, etc.

A&SP didn't always solicit sponsors to fulfill corporate needs. The news bureau produced and distributed a 225-page Press

Relations Manual that keyed on "experience, not theory." For many years, A&SP also produced and sold to company components a Writers' Manual that promoted style and usage standards.

On the initiative of A&SP's Roy Stratton, the department produced in 1981 a sure winner: "Customers Aren't Always Men, or How to Communicate More Effectively in the Changing World." It came out just in time for copywriter Janet Gutowski Hall, one-time editor of A&SP's weekly news sheet. She reported testily that a reader had written in to inquire about a GE woman's name, address, age, and "martial status."

Lewis stayed with A&SP only three years, moving on in 1975 to join Stan Smith who had left GE to become chairman of International Paper. But the legacy lingered.

Bob Pulver, his successor, made it clear that the "basic principles of Lewis" had not changed. A&SP would adhere to the disciplines of matrix management and integrated programs. Many of the programs just described, in fact, extended over both regimes.

A&SP's primary mission, stated Pulver, was still to serve operations, and it would respond to corporate "on request." There were to be no revolutionary changes, he said, although it was possible some further consolidations would be made.

Changes of degree

The two GMs were an interesting pair – so alike in some of the things they tried to do that the image of one mirrored that of the other. People often described one as "hands on" and the other as "hands off." Viewpoints varied so widely, however, that the labels fluttered back and forth between the two.

Their talents were complementary, but in a way that was contradictory. Lewis, the trained engineer, was a visionary. Pulver, who came up the creative route, was a conceptual pragmatist.

Lewis loved to postulate on end, and then prod his pupils to convert sketches into grand designs. The exercises were obtuse, but fun.

Pulver, on the other hand, preferred to craft the department in the way he learned to create ads – with logic, precision, and grace. He would need all those talents, and more, because the communications machine known as A&SP would soon face major repair work.

The problem was that the noise of an impending discontinuity was muffled by the seductive strains of "We Bring Good Things To Life."

XI THE CREATION

When the Texas executive saw our ad in The Wall Street Journal, *he had on his desk seven competitive proposals to build a cogeneration power plant. He called the 800 number in boldface at the bottom of the ad, said he was glad to know we were in the business, and asked for a GE proposal. Within a matter of months, a $200 million contract for the plant was signed, along with a 10-year commitment to fuel the plant with natural gas from Ladd Petroleum, a GE subsidiary. Total value of the order: $1.2 billion. Not bad for a direct response ad.*

The creative process was, for A&SP as for others in the industry, an endless and exhilarating quest. GE proved a fertile field for exploration.

Bob Peare, vice president of corporate PR, put it in perspective in the '40s: "GE has, from the very first, been set up to provide individuals with the opportunity to put their ideas into useful effect – to provide fulcrums, so to speak, for the levers of the mind, with which, by Archimedes' demonstration, we can move the world."

Freeing the mind

This, to A&SPers, was a license to let the mind soar. But top officers in GE made it clear early on that creative practicioners, whether doing marketing communications in A&SP or moving goods in other GE functions, should first be concerned with a sound launching pad. As GE Chairman Philip D. Reed cautioned:

"Personality has the ability to open many doors, but character must keep them open. Character is what every man seeks in another."

Years later, ex-A&SPer and GE Staff Executive Bob Fegley checked topside to see if this still squared with what CEO Reg Jones expected from GE communicators. "First," confirmed Jones, "comes integrity." Only then did he go on to such things as business sense and an understanding of key issues.

What better character for A&SP communications, then, than a reflection of GE people and GE products: Quality. Reliability. Conservatism.

In advertising, of course, this poses the danger of dullness. But with few exceptions, A&SP ignored the pitfalls and aligned its output with GE marketing thrusts, to help sell products, services, ideas, and the company.

In this, A&SP found its resolve reinforced. "Ad writers," wrote Claude Hopkins, one of the early industry giants, "forget they are salesmen and try to be performers." Bill Bernbach echoed this later when he stated: "Every ad (produced in this shop) will have a selling point. There are no exceptions to this."

In the belief, therefore, that its journey was well charted, and that its mission was ordained, A&SP set off in search of the Creative Grail. Its strategy envisioned three thrusts – one procedural, another conceptual, and a third organizational.

First strategic thrust

The first thrust brought into play a theoretical sledgehammer, based on the assumption that if you throw enough talent at a problem, you're bound to come up with something good. It was saturation vs. subtlety, almost a matter of mass versus class.

Whenever A&SP took on a big program, it assembled a large task force of experts to search for the solution. These weren't solely the "creatives" representing copy and art. Every A&SP function joined in.

Once the program strategy and theme had been defined, the fuctional teams went off to joust in their specialties. Surviving ideas were hauled back to the reassembled camp for shaping and sharing. The results were then molded into a central visual concept, usually with obligatory program logo, and packaged for client presentation.

The last Master Check List of A&SP Services issued in 1970 as a part of the Procedures Manual outlined the 16 major functions that surfaced in most major projects: program planning, space advertising, media planning, radio and TV, sales promotion, publicity, buying and selling information, audio visual, exhibits and displays, technical and service manuals, customer presentations, sales training and education, production and distribution, regional advertising and sales promotion, research, and manpower development, training and placement.

These fanned out into 161 subfunctions. Even the familiar agency services of advertising, collateral and publicity contained such refinements as Yellow Page advertising, sheets and binders for sales proposals, and A&SP-authored articles for the trade press. One of the more important categories – sales promotion – went far beyond mere brochures. It trumpeted periodicals, renewal parts bulletins, individual customer campaigns, agent and distributor programs, sales incentive and motivational programs, awards and trophies, premiums and promotional aids – on and on.

How A&SP differed from other agencies

This diversity marked the major difference between A&SP and other big communications agencies. A&SP rarely produced just ad and PR programs. A&SP created integrated programs. Planning sessions started with the full scope of A&SP services, and only those functions which weren't seen as vital in reaching program goals were eliminated.

Sometimes this worked against the normal creative tack of agencies. In 1982, as one example, the department produced a broadly integrated marketing communications program to back a new GE thrust on factory automation. The effort included extensive promotional pieces, trade show participation and audio visual presentations . . . but no space. A&SP didn't even recommend it. As A&SP Manager Bob Pulver noted, "The advertising tradition was broken, because our strategy called for a communications mix that approached our market in new ways."

Second: craft a creative concept

The second creative thrust launched by A&SP – a working concept – took a long time to complete. Its nucleus centered on the lure which brought most A&SPers to the industry: the Word.

Words gave writers the edge because, once the program strategy was settled, they were given the lead in scoping out the creative pieces. Their first output usually included thumbnail sketches, along with their words, which were passed on to layout artists for embellishment.

Incredible as this may seem today, the practice persisted in A&SP until the mid-'70s. But the department wasn't alone. In a speech to A&SP's Creative Services Operation in the mid-'70s, a BBDO senior art director acknowledged that until only a few years before, his agency did the same, in some cases actually sending the copy by internal mail from writer to artist.

This lead role was heady stuff for young A&SP writers. The problem was, it only lasted while they were young. They learned quickly that, much as they might like to write, real promotion came to copywriters only if they could unchain themselves from the basement and move up to account supervisor, or – nirvana! – Manager.

They also learned that seldom if ever did their ad or brochure ooze out from the press of bureaucratic approval in pristine glory. Hence, they either developed an incredible tolerance for compromise with honor, or moved elsewhere. Many of those who started with A&SP made the move soon.

The search for copy formulas

As one might expect in a technically oriented company such as GE, A&SP writers searched for formulas. They siphoned ideas from theorists such as Maslow and Koestler and Wallas, hitchhiked on *A Technique for Producing Ideas* by James Webb Young, and cobbled up their own literary road maps from Gallup-Robinson Advertising Impact Reports.

One of the simplest formulas fed on the workings of the engineering mind: with any technical paper, go to the last paragraph, and there is your lead. Linear logic.

One of the most enduring was a copy formula I brought to A&SP from my stay with Bozell & Jacobs at its headquarters in Omaha. The agency at that time generated billings of $20 million from 10 offices. That's the equivalent of about five cents on the dollar to what it bills today as Bozell, Jacobs, Kenyon & Eckhardt, under CEO Chuck Peebler.

When Leo Bozell and Morris Jacobs founded the agency a few years before, they were nervous about its prospects, so they retained their newspaper jobs. Bozell – on the morning paper – worked days at the agency after the paper had been put to bed; Jacobs – on the evening edition – worked nights. When I was there, they still closely minded the store, so staffers gained the benefit of their real-world wisdom.

From Bozell came perspective, via the motto on his office wall: "The sun will rise without thy assistance."

From Jacobs came compassion. During the early days of the agency, he met a young priest who had become discouraged through his work with derelict men. "It's the wrong end of the human scale," he told Jacobs. "I'm going to concentrate up front."

Jacobs agreed, and while he couldn't really afford it, he loaned the priest $90 to rent an old house to take care of five homeless boys. It was a sound investment in more ways than one. The priest was Father Flanagan, and the product of his vision, Boys Town, became the long term client of Bozell & Jacobs.

Source of the A&SP formula: Bozell & Jacobs

From one of the pros at the agency came the A&SP copy formula. Jacobs had assigned me to a crusty copy/contact rep named Jack Dow, who was B&J's agricultural specialist. First off, he showed me two ads and asked me to choose the better.

The first was jammed full of type, used splashes of orange red, and sported a bold coupon. The second one was gorgeous – big, full-color picture, short copy, lots of white space. It was the winner, hands down.

"Wrong," said Jack. And in telling me why, he outlined the formula which I later brought to A&SP. "It all starts with one person out there, not here," he said. "Put yourself in the farmer's shoes and then write the answers to his questions, which come in this order: What will it do for me? How do I know that's true? What other features does it have? Who uses it? Who makes it? How much is it? Where can I buy it?" And as for layout, he held up the more cluttered of the two ads, saying with a shrug: "Form follows function."

It was the classic direct response formula and, in fact, the classic copy formula. It played on the most powerful motivation in salesmanship (with the possible exception of the urge to change someone else's copy) – self-interest.

Beginning in 1953, the formula served as the framework for A&SP's Copywriting II course, which I conducted in 11 sessions of an hour and a half each, including lectures, exercises, homework, quizzes, the works. Trainees explored the rationale for the formula over the next 21 years under succeeding instructors until, during the Lewis era, the "How To" book took over as a bridge for the new Marketing Communications Program, then being developed.

But, what do you know – there, nestled comfortably in the midst of the 203-page "How To" book, representing the only specifics on a single page devoted to the "Techniques of Preparing Ad Copy," was the formula. Which is about as trim as words can remain after being poked and picked at by writers for more than two decades.

The general manager's own formula

Long before Bob Pulver became head of A&SP, he had developed a kind of copy formula of his own: "The essence of writing is really the ability to understand what you are writing." One was tempted to tack on an admonition from E. B. White to make Bob's formula whole: "When you say something, make sure you have said it. The chances of your having said it are only fair."

Pulver, as much as anyone in A&SP, knew how managerial duties could jeopardize the practiced skills of a writer. He lamented in 1977: "The first things to go are the aesthetics. The unity develops fissures. The flow grows turbid. The crisp word no longer springs to that special spot somewhere between your eyeballs and your vocal cords; it's overlayered with all the managerial words, the policy words, the jargon words."

While he had built his reputation as a writer, Pulver knew that words were not the sole key to creativity. In 1972, he gained both the time and charter to search for a more all-encompassing formula. Will Lewis had named Bob section guru of creativity and Pulver, in turn, assigned to the task Walt Brzoza, representing art, and Bob Lauterborn, representing copy.

The two spent six months talking with experts in agencies, the media, and client companies. They analyzed more than 100,000 readership reports. They poured over the best of the ad books. While this didn't immediately bring the Creative Grail into focus, they sighted plenty of milestones along the way.

"Avoid humor," said John Caples. "What's funny to one person isn't to millions of others. Copy should sell, not just entertain. Remember there's not one funny line in the two most influential books ever written: the Bible and the Sears catalog."

"The ad," said David Ogilvy, "should be literal, realistic, simple, direct – never symbolic or complex."

Rosser Reeves: "Make your idea so good that even a lousy layout will not kill it."

Leo Burnett: "If you want to be different for the sake of being different, you can always come down in the morning with a sock in your mouth."

And, as some of the old-time A&SPers kept reminding Pulver & Co., there were always the precepts of Stan Smith's knight in shining metaphor: the Creative Effective Advocate.

At times, people tended to dance around creativity rather than define it. David McCall, CEO of McCaffrey & McCall, in 1977 told the Association of National Advertisers: "Today, I want to talk about magic and the people who perform it." Alex Kroll of Y&R flanked the subject by warning a governmental group: "Expect creative people to show flashes of pique, nervous twitches, (and occasionally) angry retorts. They're paid to live closer to their nerve endings than you are."

Others disdained the quest. Ex-A&SPer Carlton "Corkie" Hawthorne, when at Wilson Haight & Welch in Hartford, observed: "Any survey concerning creativity is a bunch of baloney. When we won 19 of 50 awards of the Hartford Ad Club, rather than new business calls, we got 25 calls to hire away our creative department."

Creativity, it seemed, was as much a will-o'-the-wisp as justice, beauty and truth. The astute historian and philosopher Will Durant sighed about the latter three, after completing the "Story of Civilization" in 11 volumes covering 9,965 pages: "Perhaps none of these can be defined."

The core of creativity: Leo Burnett

Yet Walt and Bob felt the irrepressible Burnett had plumbed the core of the question when he said: "I have always felt that perhaps the real key to this nebulous thing called 'creativity' is the art of establishing new and meaningful relationships between previously unrelated things." In an afterthought that hitchhiked on Durant, he noted this should be done "in a manner that is relevant, believable and in good taste, but which somehow presents the product in a fresh, new light."

This formed the foundation for the Guidelines for Creativity which Brzoza soon codified for A&SP: "Creativity is just a new combination of ideas already in your mind. It is relating unrelated thoughts."

Simple. Elegant. Powerful. Yet not quite a formula. As Gertrude Stein once said, it had a certain syrup, but it didn't pour.

So Walt and Bob delved into the dozens of formulas in use – Ted Bates' Unique Selling Proposition, Benton & Bowles' Creative Work Plan, N. W. Ayres' Workbook, Al Ries' and Jack Trout's Positioning, McCann-Erickson's Advertising Strategy, and so on.

Bringing things into FOCUS

From this, they forged A&SP's FOCUS concept, which they summarized in three key words: *Dramatize* a *Proposition* to a *Receiver.* "Repeat these words until you know them backwards," they told A&SPers, "because that's the way the formula works."

The trigger point for any successful appeal, they concluded, was self-interest. It was the touchstone of every creative formula they had uncovered, including the A&SP transplant from Jack Dow at Bozell & Jacobs. The principle was timeless. As early as 160 B.C., the Roman playwright Terence had noted: "Of all mankind, each loves himself the best."

FOCUS, therefore, started with the Receiver. The first step, which was analytical, called for A&SPers to pin down this being – not some nameless, mindless audience, but a single, composite personality – and to jot down the Receiver's wants and needs, ranging beyond the product itself.

Step two – switching now to strategic thinking – brought A&SPers to the Proposition, which was usually framed by the writer. This, they discovered, was not the headline or theme, nor the objective, nor even a selling proposition. Instead, it was a single, strategic statement which bridged the gap between what GE wanted to say and what the prospect wanted to hear. In effect, it answered the eternal question of the Receiver: "What will it do for me?"

Only when those two steps were taken did writer and artist go on to the fun part – Dramatization. FOCUS stipulated two rules.

To begin with, Dramatization was not merely a matter of decorating the copy; rather, it meant visually supporting the Proposition in a way that enhanced the impact on the Receiver. Then – and this was by far the most important contribution of FOCUS to A&SP – it spelled the end of the creative bucket brigade. Now, both writer and artist grasped the Proposition so that jointly they could hoist it to new heights.

By design, the copy in most cases had not yet been written. But creative synergy soon surged, so that headline and illustration reinforced each other. As Lauterborn said of the process: "Writers make artists articulate; artists give writers vision."

The FOCUS concept and Brzoza's *Guidelines for Creativity* were drummed into A&SPers in classrooms, booklets and work sessions. Most who learned it and put it to use, liked the concept because it worked. Some old-line GE ad managers disagreed. As one told his A&SP account rep: "If you want to talk to the Receiver, make *him* pay for it."

The clients' view of FOCUS

Most clients, however, favored it for a couple of reasons. First, they recognized that FOCUS built on universal principles and could be applied to any of their communications. And second, they liked the kinship it shared with a revered GE trait: discipline.

A&SP reviewed FOCUS with more than 500 GE people, and it was broadly endorsed. It helped, in part, that it matched the concept envisioned for the GE strategic planning process in the mid-1970s by Senior Vice President Charles Reed: "We don't want to delude ourselves, so we are using customers' perceptions – not ours – as the gauge of whether or not we have anything unique to offer."

A&SP thereafter promoted the concept for all work, and set up FOCUS awards to recognize exceptional execution. This honored clients as well as A&SP contributors, and extended beyond ads and sales promotion to all communications functions.

The initial result, as expected, was better integration of copy and art and, therefore, higher impact on Receivers. Even outsiders liked the result. One competitor used the A&SP-produced "Guide to Prevention and Repair of Motor and Generator Failure" brochure so often to illustrate its own service for customers that A&SP finally had to reprint it with a GE logo on each page.

A GE sales engineer also lavished praise on a FOCUS-oriented piece for engineering structural foam: "It's the best handbook I've seen in 20 years . . . the first brochure I ever saw get a standing ovation . . . may be the best technical brochure in the company today."

Some flights of creativity went unrecognized. For example, I have always regretted not giving an award to Bill Muir, now CEO of Muir Cornelius Moore in New York City. Bill came to me late one Friday to explain why he could not work that weekend on a crash project: "I'll be parachute jumping at West Point," he said.

I did not press for details. It would have spoiled the effect.

FOCUS did not preclude using copy formulas. The A&SP formula had worked earlier on a GE locomotive ad that led to a sale, so I used it again with Art Director Sal Cascio on a series of single-page, black and white ads, again with coupons, for industrial turbines. A manager at Philip Morris – not yet identified as a prospect by either field sales or the product department – sent in for the evaluation offered, and placed a $4 million order. Reported the client in Lynn, Bill Folsom: "It's a provable instance where advertising caused a result to occur that never would have happened without it. We like that kind of support from our agency."

I used the copy formula to write the $1.2 billion cogeneration plant ad in *The Wall Street Journal.* All ads, of course, are the product of more than words. The copy was bolstered by the account work of Dick Huether and Debby Hoyt, by the art direction of Dick Stahl, and by a headline I cribbed from Dave Jones: "Energy can add to the cost of your product or add to the profit of your company. The difference is cogeneration."

Even the client earned his pay the day the ad appeared. Ed Phelps, now CEO of Norfield Corp. in Danbury, CT, was at the time general manager of GE's Cogeneration Applications Department in Schenectady. He decided to test the response a reader would get by calling the 800 number in the ad. He sat bolt upright when a bubbly young voice at the answering service greeted him with: "GE Cogenitals!" Since he was the first to call, he set things straight.

Third thrust: organizational

For its third creative thrust, A&SP unlimbered various organizational tactics.

For many years, A&SP account supervisors had led the charge, reinforced by copywriters assigned to them as well as artists from a central pool. These point squads were free to create at will, subject only to the countermands of the subsection manager, the section manager, the department general manager, and Planning Board. And, of course, clients and lawyers.

Over time, some subsections began to form their own creative pools. These, they found, made it easier to balance workloads between account teams and, though it hadn't been planned, to match the talents of A&SPers with their interests.

The catalyst for the latter was A&SP's host organization, the Industrial Sales Division. When it had trouble recruiting sales engineers in the '60s, it turned to Liberal Arts graduates to fill the gap. So A&SP decided to try the same. It loosened creative standards and went after the All-American boy (girls weren't prime recruiting targets yet). This assumed that generalists rather than specialists could adapt more easily to the broad demands of rotating assignments. The pools came in handy, because

A&SPers who wanted to write or draw drifted there naturally, while the Jack Armstrongs opted for the accounts.

When A&SP centralized its creative and account sections in 1957, the department hoped to further accommodate the interest of its people while improving creative output. In fact, it did neither.

Matching talent to function

The usual turf battles stemming from reorganization made it hard for the new sections to match talent with function. Creatives who did break loose from accounts found it more difficult than ever to do creative work.

That was pre-FOCUS, of course, so copywriters not only created apart from artists but apart from account reps. The latter found that a request for a job disappeared down the creative maw where it was chewed, digested and regurgitated by whichever copywriter happened to be handy.

Account reps faced other barriers in their work. Technically they were responsible for all work produced for their assigned clients. But none of them really succeeded in getting A&SP support troops to line up behind them in lockstep. As a consequence, account reps spent much of their time presenting work that didn't match their expectations, or deciphering reports from finance. This was pre-computer, and many of the 17 monthly reports per account were prepared by hand.

Often, the result was chaos. The effectiveness and level of creative work plummeted. Many creatives who had envisioned account sections as their window of advancement found, instead, that they were mired in the muck of accounting and frustration.

It was the A&SP Al Ries once referred to as "the place where GE's old-line utility and industrial product divisions went when they wanted to buy advertising that looked cheap."

Ultimately, reality set in and A&SP settled back on its traditional course. Small creative pools re-formed at headquarters. The branches, while calling on Schenectady for critical-mass services and help on overwhelming projects, created their own pools which were shored up by free lancers and local specialty houses.

By the early '70s, good-sized creative pools again gained respectability. Jack Dumas formed one for his electronic and aerospace section, naming Bob Pulver to head it. Roy Stratton, whom Will Lewis had spirited back to A&SP from GE corporate, formed another to serve his section-wide needs in energy systems.

When Lewis became general manager in 1972, he bodily removed Pulver and staff from Dumas' area to form the new, free-floating group that developed FOCUS and offered creative support to anyone in A&SP. Three years later, Pulver moved up to head A&SP. Since the program manager concept instituted by Lewis seemed to be working well, Bob decided once more to go all the way in centralizing creative. This time, he crafted with care.

Everybody into the pool

The new operation, called Creative Services, included all A&SP creatives plus production support, and AVCOM. To head the new section, Pulver named A&SP's consummate professional manager – Roy Stratton. He brought impeccable specs to the post.

Roy was creative in his own right, having paid his dues, as he liked to recount, as copywriter during the '50s "on the weary benches." He therefore understood the problems of the lowliest creatives. He had also comfortably maneuvered among top management on Madison Avenue and among execs at the highest levels of GE, in his role as corporate ad manager.

Because of that experience, Roy made sure A&SP's creative output steered closely to the course of corporate. This meant adhering to GE's position on public issues – nuclear, environmental, defense, etc. – and, most of all, to the proper use of the GE monogram and signature.

The sheer volume of A&SP work helped make the trademark and trade name among the most recognized in the U.S. and, therefore, among the most valuable. At least one counterfeiter agreed, printing up a batch of bogus $20 bills with the GE monogram replacing the Federal Reserve seal. He assumed, as reported in GE Trademark Topics, the mark was so familiar no one would notice.

The GE logo also became an irresistible target for creatives. Artists in particular were forever trying to tilt it, color it, redesign it – anything that in their minds improved it.

Stan Smith had dramatized the issue when he took over corporate advertising and public relations. The monogram is inviolable, he said, and re-stated a dictum he had instilled throughout A&SP: "There is no maximum size to the GE signature." To make his point, Smith always sent a ruler along with a copy of the infraction to the production person. To most art directors, Stan's charter meant "The bigger, the horsier." So they plotted ways around it.

Stratton had sensed as corporate ad manager, including time under Smith, that the art directors at BBDO had somehow succeeded. On instinct, he pulled file copies of their ads for GE and, ruler in hand, confirmed his hunch. Imperceptibly, but measurably year after year, they had shrunk the size of the GE signature until it met their standards. Roy concluded, being as much a realist as a loyalist, that no harm had been done and that, in fact, BBDO's product looked pretty good.

Polishing the monogram

Roy also made sure that A&SP proudly held aloft, along with the GE signature, the corporate slogan of the moment. During GE's first century, surprisingly few surfaced and those that did, reflected the company's conservatism.

Beginning in the '40s, the banner proclaimed, "You can put your confidence in General Electric." This gave way in the mid-'50s to one of the most recognized of all GE slogans, "Progress is our most important product."

It became apparent as the '60s wore down, that "Progress" didn't properly reflect the company's growing social consciousness. So throughout the '70s GE experimented with others. Among them: the short-lived "Men helping Man," and a transitory compromise, "Progress for People." None of them caught on quite like a new one introduced by GE Consumer, "We bring good things to life."

A Trendex study suggested that corporate could do worse than reincarnate "Progress is our most" etc. Twelve years after it had last been used, it still earned 40% awareness among adults, the same gained by the fledgling "Good Things."

In hewing to the corporate line, Roy resolved to reap the classic benefits of decentralization. He planted A&SP creative centers in the five principal A&SP business locations – Albany, Stamford, Washington, Chicago, and Louisville. He nurtured growth by giving each creative director full operating freedom, subject only to corporate and A&SP business guidelines, including FOCUS.

Unleashing five creative centers

Each office formed, in effect, a free-wheeling, fast-moving agency that mapped out for its own a gigantic arc of the GE universe. Within this, creative and account people became true peers, spending as much time in client orbit as in their own. In that context, they gauged satisfaction as much in solving business problems as in creating communications, and in the process did well at both.

They rarely became enmeshed in political skirmishes, because Stratton spent most of his time in that arena, fending and fostering on their behalf. He encouraged networking, whereby the offices swapped creatives to balance workload and share unique skills. He convened quarterly seminars that brought together everyone in the same function to hone skills. Writers, for example, explored the Word with NBC's Edwin Newman, who winced as he recalled the library notice in Colorado boasting of its "bibliography of books" and "volumes of easy difficulty."

Roy also published and distributed the best of his people's work, plus GE output from areas of the company not served by A&SP, in eight brochures on *Contemporary Communications Standards.* Any student or practitioner can still mine rich veins of ideas in the set, which ranged over ads and brochures to TV and radio spots to press relations and executive speech writing.

Spearheading GE business thrusts

In the sweep of A&SP's recorded history, this was for creatives the Hellenistic Era or, at least, the Age of the Antonines. From the outposts as well as the commmand center, fully integrated programs marched forth in majestic regularity as the phalanx for GE business thrusts.

From Albany came a promotional salvo so compelling that a consortium of 30 utilities used it as their agenda in evaluating steam turbines, concluding with a $400 million order for four GE units.

Stamford launched "Two for the Road," a sales incentive program which outflanked 250 competitors by prompting 7,500 inside and outside salespersons to exceed their GE sales budgets.

A $100,000 advertising and PR program initiated in Japan by Washington created, according to the client, "the climate for All Nippon Airways to comfortably propose the CF6 engine for 747s." As a side benefit, A&SP captured $220,000 in airline allowance advertising for the carrier.

Schenectady targeted 65,500 registrants at the Offshore Technology Conference with live product demos that gained $3.4 million in sales leads at less than half the national average cost per visitor.

Pittsfield helped boost the sale of Valox plastics 35% in less than a year. Campbell helped see that GE didn't lose a single reactor fuel channel replacement order during the course of its campaign. And Louisville served up the press to major appliances with a cooking school conducted by Paul Prudhomme, famed Creole food authority, in the New Orleans Superdome.

From Phoenix came word of another sort: "Stop running the ad on computer service. Our people can't keep up with the inquiries." But not headquarters: an A&SP-produced color spread promoting on-site machining generated a $2 million order through *Industry Week* and another for $200,000 from a vertical trade. While the ad targeted results, it also snagged a "World's Best" Business/Professional Advertising Association international ranking, dubbed by Pulver "the most prestigious award in the business advertising field."

Even VP of corporate PR Doug Moore, to whom A&SP had been assigned in 1974, sent along to Pulver his feeling about A&SP output: "Great!"

Perhaps the ultimate accolade came from the least likely source. James F. Bell, Industrial Sales Division counsel, wrote: "The reams of literature crossing my desk can quickly make one jaded." But upon reviewing Take The Burlington Route, a sales incentive program for switchgear made in Burlington, Iowa, he noted, "I had to take a moment to express my admiration for a job excellently done, both in concept and execution."

Pax Romana.

In 1980, however, A&SP's peaceful cadence was jolted when the department was reassigned to Corporate Consulting Services. While the CCS vice president, Marian Kellogg, was considered a management expert and was the author of several books, she expressed no strong opinion of A&SP, good or bad. But she did relay an opinion that overrode anything she might have thought: A&SP, according to the Corporate Executive Office, "wasn't very creative."

One had to read this in the context of analyzing the Receiver. There may be no problem, but if the Receiver perceives you have a problem, then you *have* a problem.

The importance of being creative

What to do? A&SP concluded it must raise its sights. And when it did, management thought it detected, high on the ramparts of Fairfield, the faint outlines of a motto that later became rampant throughout industry: Less is More.

Jack Welch had come on scene six months after Kellogg's arrival. While he made no immediate move that affected A&SP,

his actions mirrored his philosophy: staffing should come from fewer, but higher level professionals.

The A&SP training program, therefore, seemed not only academic but counter-productive. A&SP began to phase it out and to shift training to program managers. Recruiting targeted professional hires only. A&SP also developed a new Quality System which programmed improvement in all A&SP functions, including creativity. In some respects it surpassed in detail the ancient A&SP Procedures Manual.

Four months after Welch became chairman, another clue to conduct beamed down from corporate. "We bring good things to life" was to be used throughout the company.

The slogan had been developed by BBDO for a flight of TV spots for GE major appliances. In this case, the creative strategy didn't hinge on the logic of a formula. As Phil Dusenberry, chairman and CEO of BBDO New York, later told *The New York Times,* "In an age when most products aren't very different, the difference is often in the way people feel about the product." That approach, said the *Times* in critiquing BBDO's output, is "epitomized in another Dusenberry campaign, for General Electric – warm, homey, images of bringing 'good things to life.' "

The GE major appliance ad chief and client for "We bring good things to life" was Len Vickers. He had been lured away from BBDO where he headed the GE consumer account by Jack Welch, who at the time was in charge of GE's $5 billion consumer business.

The birth of We Bring Good Things to Life

BBDO had trouble developing WBGTTL, according to *Madison Avenue* magazine. The agency wasn't sure if Vickers just wanted a new theme line or something that would change the stodgy GE image. The heart of his charter: don't talk about what we make; talk about who we are. When Vickers saw BBDO's proposal wrapped around "We bring good things to life," he knew it would work, even though he didn't quite know why. "To recognize The Big Idea," he said, "takes either extreme experience or sweet ignorance. You must be able to respond at the viewer level with informed naivety."

TV viewers, not privy to the trauma of birth, judged the spots and slogan by what they saw and felt and remembered. They took an immediate liking to the offspring from Vickers' vision and Dusenberry's philosophy. And fortunately, the one Receiver who maybe didn't personify the rest but nevertheless counted more than all the others – Jack Welch – liked them, too.

A&SPers did their best to fold "We bring good things to life" into their work. Internationally, it created problems. In Arabic, for example, the theme translated "We raise your ancestors from the dead." With GE defense products, such as the re-entry warhead for ICBMs, it was ludicrous to even consider it. The theme also proved a non sequitur for some industrial lines. How much credibility could one buy, for example, by hanging it on GE switchgear, which looked like a YMCA locker and had about as much sex appeal?

None of these actions came to grips with the core issue: A&SP's perceived creativity. Results alone, Pulver concluded, were no longer enough. So he proposed to the Corporate Executive Office a solution: A&SP will "concentrate all advertising work under an advertising director."

The favorable response meant one thing: A&SP could now put in place people who could produce creative work of the type corporate was used to getting.

Creative solution: recruit in the Big City

The source of that kind of talent, of course, was the Big City – i.e., Madison Avenue. In a rare game of musical chairs, Roy Stratton in the Fall of 1981 participated in recruiting his own successor before moving on to a new challenge in the resources section. There, he directed 120 specialists in producing all the esoteric forms of A&SP collateral, other than print promotion.

A&SP's new creative director in Norwalk, Ted French, had most recently been VP-Management Supervisor/Creative Director at Marsteller in New York City. Ironically, his Madison Avenue credentials were bolstered by a tour of duty with the A&SP expatriates at Muller Jordan Herrick, and by rubbing shoulders in the early '60s at Marsteller with ex-A&SPer Al Ries.

At first, only modest changes were made. FOCUS expanded to something called the FOCUS Strategy System. This still paid respects to the Receiver and the Proposition. But it borrowed heavily from various systems used by major agencies, highlighting such things as the Key Fact, Mandatories, Policy Limitations, and the Problem Advertising Must Solve, which A&SP now labelled Selling Against.

The invulnerable Time Sheet

Writers and artists heard with pleasure that creative costs were to "change from liquidation to overhead" – i.e., the eternal time sheet was to be dumped ... which of course never happened.

They learned the advertising buzz words currently popular on The Street, such as Closure, and Discovery. A&SP creatives also were drilled in a 14-page profile of the GE Personality, aimed at building the GE brand while promoting GE products. While this responded to Welch's call to become "better than the best," it flip-flopped FOCUS, turning from an analytical view of the Receiver to a Utopian view of the Sender. The portrait was drawn by GE in advance of sending, instead of by the customer, in the wake of receiving.

Then in mid-1982, in a move which signalled that not only the Big City but the Big Time had come to A&SP, the department was assigned to Corporate Marketing. Vickers already had the old corporate advertising and PR group to help sharpen his vision, and corporate consulting to shore up his strategy. Now, he had A&SP to help flex his wings if that were his choice.

A&SP was modestly trimmed in the process. The news bureau was permanently transferred to a new staff component, Corporate Public Relations, while Ralph MacLachlan's distribution services – along with its magical, budget-making cash cow, the warehouse – went to Corporate Production Services.

The breeze from Vickers' entrance blew hot and cold.

A&SPers were delighted to find that earlier in his career he had hoped to become a writer. "I have enormous respect for effective, creative people," he had said. Surely, then, he would empathize with those who felt the creative process was much as described by sports columnist Red Smith: "There's nothing to it – you just put paper in the typewriter, sit there until beads of blood form on your brow, and write."

They were not happy, however, when he proclaimed that henceforth A&SP was to be known as the Corporate Industrial Advertising Operation. The Corporate was acceptable, they concluded, but not Industrial. It smacked too much of Andy Jackson at the Battle of New Orleans, who commanded: "Boys, let us elevate them guns a little lower." And, as anyone with an ounce of prescience knew, CIAO in Italian meant "goodbye."

Even the press speculated that something was up. In August of 1982, the lead banner in *Advertising Age* blared: "GE's famed ad shop being closed Sept. 1." Pulver countered with a letter to the troops: "Not so." Yet two months later, he announced that it was necessary to "respond to the recent fall-off in demand for advertising and promotion services." By year end, the outlying offices in Vienna, Oak Brook, Louisville and Campbell were to be closed. Added Pulver: "Work will be transferred to Norwalk."

Vickers redefines the A&SP mission

What this called for, more than anything else, was a re-definition of A&SP's mission. Before long, building blocks in random dimensions began falling in place.

The first thud was encouraging. A&SP got a new name: Corporate Marketing Communications Operation.

Next came word that A&SP would concentrate on bigger programs that were broadly integrated. Systems sell was to take precedence over product promotion. A&SP had recognized Vickers' interest in major programs before he took over the department. Early in 1982, A&SP had gone to him for Corporate Marketing's endorsement of new A&SP initiatives on factory automation and information services. Playback to creatives from one attending A&SPer: "Believe we're on a roll."

Later that year, with A&SP under his wing, Vickers reported that Welch had lauded A&SP programs presented at a security analysts meeting. At the same time, Vickers vowed to make GE creative standards, over the long term, "the best in the world."

A&SPers were delighted to join this latest crusade in the cause. But bravado buckled when they heard him proclaim his line of march: to "go outside." With discouraging regularity, A&SP saw Vickers review a parade of programs from BBDO, Marsteller, Chiat Day, a Swedish agency, and others. A New York City shop named after its principal, Jim Johnston, Inc., was later signed on for a corporate print campaign in the business press.

The advertising section still smarted from comments on high that A&SP was "not creative" and vowed to correct this image.

Initially, creative salvos were lobbed to Vickers from A&SP outposts as well as Norwalk. There weren't many direct hits. A Less is More systems campaign from Albany was called "insensitive." Programs came back from other offices for re-work or, worse, with no clear charter. As frustration mounted, the advertising section decided to tighten the reins so that all sorties launched would carry the clear stamp of Norwalk as to tone and style.

The outer office closings simplified the task. Fortress Norwalk was to be bolstered by a "strong, ongoing, on-site Albany creative operation." But it never really came about. The work force there was culled, and recruiting from the Big Time faltered. As New York City recruiter Frank Wulff later rued: "The most difficult job I ever had was to hire a good writer for Albany. I tried for years and never got one."

Thereafter, all work was forced through a firmly drawn creative die in Norwalk. Strategy and pieces were reviewed there and, in most cases, refined to rigid standards. Major programs were assigned there. Jobs retained in Albany were produced to detailed specs from Norwalk: seamless paper for photo backgrounds; wrap-around type to balance a multitude of small photos against a major one; etc.

The price of creativity

Seemingly, the Grail was in sight. Creative execution was usually clever, often brilliant, and consistently high in quality.

But it came at a price. It was as if the U.S. government had decided to cast all states in the mold of California. While the spell of the redwood and the palm was enduring, one hankered on occasion for a flash of maple, the daintiness of dogwood, even the rustle of leaves on a corn stalk.

And it forever changed the creative complexion of A&SP. The license to soar was gone. One mourned that writers and artists could no longer be encouraged to dream up a coloring book as a sales primer, a full-size cut-out suit for an incentive mailing program, or an ad series that featured Broom Hilda peddling GE industrial component products.

Nor could one ever again expect to regenerate the single-minded devotion to A&SP of an art director like Sal Cascio – bringing him, as Walt Brzoza and Dick Savage once did, to the Saratoga Raceway, where they showed Sal a listing of horses and, pointing to one line, asked for his view. To which Sal replied: "That's 6 point Helvetica. I'd move the line down. It needs more lead."

A&SP creative attention at this point focused almost entirely on ads. If results were out as a measure of creativity, awards were surely in. The lead headline of A&SP's *Newsmakers*, published by the advertising section, intoned the fact, issue after issue: "T700 Black Hawk ad and Robotics publicity win Nutmegger trophies." "Programmable Controller campaign strikes silver in Effie awards competition." "Albany program brings home DMA Echo award." "Norwalk quartet performs beautifully at Matty competition." "AEBG+EPCOT+CMCO= another major award."

Worst of all was the seeming indifference outside A&SP to whether the output was good or bad. Most product departments served by the now-defunct branches learned that A&SP could not realistically handle their needs from Norwalk, and went their own ways. Clients near headquarters tended to hang on with A&SP but resented the rigid creative control, rising costs, and the obvious upward focus of A&SP management.

Actually, most clients had more important things in marketing to worry about. These usually surfaced in forced budget cuts, with two major expense line items sharing the bad news – marketing's people budget, and the ad budget. Anybody in the industrial ad business knows who wins that one.

Dark day for A&SP creatives

In time, it became obvious that while there was no approbation upstairs, there was not complete indifference.

On A&SP's Darkest Day (actually, it was July first and one of the few sunny days in the Northeast during the middle of 1985), A&SP creatives were ushered into conference rooms in Norwalk and Albany, lined up and, figuratively, shot. Every last one.

This wasn't a vendetta against creatives. Everybody else in A&SP, with the exception of a few programs people and resource specialists in exhibits, were lined up and shot, too.

A&SPers realized they were in good company, around the company, and throughout industry. It was the beginning of Downsizing to Stay Competitive. Even so, it felt better to blame all the shooting on the ubiquitous "They." Each volley, at all levels, was preceded with those words which were becoming so familiar in GE: "I hate to do this but *they* tell me I have to . . ."

Eddie Sochor pegged this tactic when he was an artist back in Albany. The firing squads had not yet formed, but the snipers were warming up on creatives, as had been their practice since the first A&SPer wrote the first GE ad. So often the bad news came down because "they" didn't like this, or "they" wanted to change that. Eddie decided to ease the way for the reviewer and raise the flag for the creator. So he designed and had printed up a classy letterhead with the single word on the masthead: *They.*

It would be the ideal way to let people in the corporate world know that their Lack of Work notice, while maybe not palatable, was nothing personal.

XII THE RENAISSANCE

"Thinking is harder than writing" – Hubert M. "Bart" Snider, A&SP Mgr. of Business Communication and Media Planning, 1985.

Near the end of the sixth decade of the 20th century, the influence of A&SP extended over the fairest part of the General Electric Company.

Under the firm and benevolent guidance of management, the department kept pace with the company in both growth and prosperous condition during a period of nearly two-score years. The far-flung talents of A&SPers were called upon in some fashion by each of the company's 170 decentralized operating departments, which were busy churning out 200,000 different models and sizes of products, spanning 3,000 different categories, in 280 plants in 33 states and 23 countries.

Throughout the corporate empire, GE marketing, sales and ad managers as a matter of course turned daily to A&SP for support functions. These ranged all the way from integrated marketing programs to the automated collation of handbook sheets by a 100-foot-long mechanical marvel at Maqua, or photography by A&SP specialists such as Jack "One Shot" McCrindle.

The resources of A&SP, honed to laser sharpness in the '70s, seemed in perfect balance with the communications needs of GE.

Elsewhere, something as mundane as the plant newspaper at the Philadelphia Works seemed to GE about as efficient as one could hope for. An A&SP account manager, arriving one day for a client call, saw this item in the early morning news sheet at the reception desk: "To the person who owns the car in the parking lot with license number NRC-9962 – your motor is running."

Back in Schenectady, a tank truck rumbled through the streets of Rotterdam emblazoned with the label "G.E. Champagne." It wouldn't have taken much to convince A&SPers who saw it that it was not the name of a local hauling firm, but instead was one more sign that the diamond inventors at the R&D Center, having achieved gem quality, were off on an interesting new tack.

Nudging a few years into the '80s, an A&SP program manager in the Washington office discovered with utter disbelief that he would have to fill out a four-page FOCUS Creative Input form before he could place a client order for business cards. And in Pittsfield, an A&SP account manager ruefully reported to his client that the estimated cost to produce matchbooks, imprinted with only three typeset words in two colors, was $2 per book.

What went wrong? What caused the process of decay that in a few short years brought on the fall of A&SP? How could this unique, respected agency decline and founder at the very time GE Chairman Jack Welch assigned it to Len Vickers, patron of the widely admired "We Bring Good Things to Life," and asked him to create a Marketing Renaissance?

The fall of A&SP came not so much from a single major misstep as from a series of minor stumbles. Each, at the time, made eminent tactical sense. Together, at the end, they spelled strategic disaster.

The first wobble appeared in 1971 when General Manager Will Lewis convinced upper management that A&SP should shift from profit and loss to cost recovery. And why not? The department had made the celestial leap the year before when it moved from operations, as a part of Industrial Sales, to staff, as a part of Consulting Services. Since it now was a corporate component, it certainly had the right to act like one.

The transitional road seemed solid enough. No longer would A&SP managers have to worry about a P&L target. All they had to do now was break even. The decrease in net would be gravy; A&SP could use it as it saw fit. The options were enticing.

Option: a competitive edge

A&SP could cut prices, of course, and gain a competitive edge over outsiders. This didn't promise much leverage, because the department's prices had always been higher than local agencies and lower than Big City shops. Price cuts mostly worked in favor of low-end business which, since A&SP had just been elevated to corporate, wasn't all that attractive.

So A&SP did just what the U.S. auto makers did when the falling dollar gave them a leg up on the Japanese. Management opted to forego any gain in market share, and live a little. For openers, A&SP did the obvious – it fixed up old offices and equipment and, where possible, breached factory walls to set up shop outside in the other world.

Most investments were not frivolous. A&SP spent the bulk of its profit windfall on futures: additional staff that fostered planning; sophisticated studies that opened the door to higher management; computerized tools that prioritized functional pieces; and a training program that for the first time leaned outward more than inward.

Some worried that, since A&SP no longer contributed to GE earnings, operating departments wouldn't respect it as much. Others pooh-poohed the thought. As those inside GE had been telling each other for years, what GE people did centered around just so much "Chinese money." A&SP charges to product departments were nothing more than electronic transactions, known within the company as Second Class Billing – far removed from the real thing.

A&SP management felt it had actually strengthened its position with clients. During the '60s, it had billed itself as "More Than An Agency," offering to do whatever anyone in GE needed, at all levels. It was then, in effect, Everyman's (or Woman's) agency. Now, in no more time than it took to reprint an organization chart, A&SP graduated, in its own mind at least, to the Thinking Man's (or Woman's) agency, dealing at higher levels on more prestigious issues.

This led to a second miscalculation in direction. As A&SP basked in the aura of corporate, it tilted more and more from the traditional agency do-it mode to that of the consultant. The resulting roadblock was labelled STAFF.

The trouble with staff

The trouble with staff, of course, is that it's perceived as overhead and makes a component visible and vulnerable. When A&SP encountered the first belt-tightening as a part of corporate in 1977, it found itself locked in with a manpower ceiling of 399. From that point on, its headcount never again went up, only down.

The easiest way to keep below the ceiling, A&SP decided, was to prune functions. In the doing, it learned that lopping off operations, such as the photo house and the typing bureau, was painless – except for the people who got lopped off. The services were readily available on the outside.

Product departments had a term for this technique – they called it "sourcing." It solved a multitude of problems – manpower ceilings, overloads, built-in cost pressures, and so forth. One simply got rid of one's problems by finding a place to have things done elsewhere, usually outside.

Sourcing created some obvious pitfalls for A&SP. Since it was apparent the department could shed operations with little effect, it became difficult to make the case that those remaining were indispensable. A&SP also found it harder to produce integrated programs when it had to go outside more and more for specialized services. Therefore, it was less inclined to propose them.

A&SP concluded that for its immediate problems, sourcing was an expedient solution. But it reluctantly realized it was also a tool with which higher management could wreak devastation downstream. This became apparent when it was later used on A&SP. Then, management didn't bother with any euphemism such as "sourcing." It called it what it really was – a simple question of Make vs. Buy.

Flirting with Parkinson's Law

A&SP generated further signs of decay in the late '70s and early '80s when it flirted with Parkinson's Law No. 6: "A perfection of planned layout is achieved only by institutions on the point of collapse."

GE components had long been subject to regulations that rivalled the military. A&SP added others to the point where its managers felt lucky if they could deviate from management duties a fraction of the time to practice individual specialties.

To begin with, A&SP managers had to drill employees on GE policies ranging from Conflict of Interest and Anti-Trust to Affirmative Action and Trade Names – even a policy issued in 1981 on Policies. Most of these spawned compliance forms which managers then had to monitor for annual updating.

A&SP managers also were expected to school the troops on department policies and procedures: Purchasing, Retainers, Gifts, Loss Due to Errors, etc., etc.

A&SP rigidly structured its operating routines. Regularly, management siphoned estimated operating cost figures, offset by sales, from account to unit to subsection to section to department and so on up.

Managers filled out complex rating sheets on all employees – two-page general appraisals on company forms, and critical evaluations on six-page A&SP forms. Each A&SPer also had to complete a seven-step manpower development plan. These flowed up the channels for perusal, back down again for revision, up for final approval and, ultimately, down for review by managers with the individuals.

Any change, which was frequent, caused reverberations like a hammer to the plumbing. Shock waves moved up and down, level by level; work quivered in suspension until the blockage was removed.

The perils of perfection

As the '80s progressed, A&SP added other refinements. FOCUS expanded analytically. All work had to be launched through a computer estimating system, then filtered, from account to production, through the new Quality System. A several-year effort was begun to monitor costs through a new Project Control system. Program managers developed strategy plans with objectives and account tactics measured against those of the department. These, along with over-all plans and policies, were screened through a new A&SP advisory board, made up of 11 key communications managers from all of the GE product sectors.

For a time, all ads and brochures under preparation were reviewed by the general manager. Program managers also could not commit to cost or time for clients without agreement of the A&SP people who would do the work. This, along with the hiring freeze, limited flexibility, adding people problems to those of pricing.

And then there were meetings – regular status and operating reviews at each level, cross-office meets, quarterly get-togethers for the whole department, sometimes the same with clients, etc. There were also training meetings on site and career development meetings both inside and outside the company.

Perhaps the ultimate meeting came in the early '80s when A&SP discovered it had incurred a 30% loss on a catalog which billed in the high six figures. To conduct a post mortem, A&SP invited 12 people off site for cocktails and dinner preceded by – a day-long meeting.

People from free-wheeling outside agencies could scarcely imagine this buttoned-up precision. But it was not unusual within a first-line, old-time *Fortune* 500 company. And as so often is the case, it threatened to transform GE strengths into muscle-bound rigidity.

A&SP's striving for perfection, in retrospect, was most likely a form of self-protection. It anticipated the most dangerous of all detours on the way to the future: change. The posture reflected the company's traditional, conservative pace of business which, as CEO Reg Jones noted in 1978, centered on a "preference for evolutionary change."

But now, a few years later, new CEO Welch proclaimed a different view: "The world is on fire with change." During a major interview in 1985, he told *The New York Times:* "Sometimes I want to shake people and say, 'Wait, a minute, the world is a different place.'"

Then Welch defined the coming: "Most bureaucracies – and ours is no exception – unfortunately still think in incremental terms rather than in terms of fundamental change. They think incrementally primarily because they think internally. Changing the culture – opening it up to quantum change – means constantly asking not how fast am I going, how well am I doing vs. how well I did a year or two before, but rather, how fast and how well am I doing vs. the world outside."

Changes under Welch

If A&SPers didn't get that message, they surely did when Welch began to implement the fundamental changes he had in mind.

The rationale: economic growth had slacked off at the time new overseas competitors were beginning to nip at the heels of U.S. firms. This forced faster innovation along with shorter product life cycles. Customers now wanted solutions from suppliers, not just products. The ticket for winning or even staying in the game was higher quality along with lower cost.

Since GE was noted for quality, Welch aimed at getting cost out. To that end, he slimmed, sloughed and de-layered.

By the end of 1985, less than five years after he took over as CEO, Welch had trimmed GE's payroll by more than 100,000 people – one quarter of GE's total. He faced these key issues sooner than most because he had to – GE was in such a diverse number of businesses that it was, in effect, a microcosm of the GNP.

By 1985, many leading *Fortune* 500 companies had decided they'd better take action, too. DuPont shed 11,200 workers through an early retirement option. The next year, AT&T announced a plan to cut 27,400 jobs. IBM, which like the old GE hardly ever fired anyone, allowed as how it might retire 10,000. And the biggest monolith of them all admitted that size could be a drawback. General Motors said it might have to boost layoffs from 40,000 to 100,000 to stay competitive.

A&SPers were surprised to find that peer companies admired Welch for his swift action. Of course, kudos varied with kinship: the higher in their organization, the greater the admiration. Those who got caught in the squeeze at the bottom, reported one GE sales rep, expressed the universal reaction: "What a crummy company to work for."

The shape of things to come

Welch reshaped GE to his own vision. The divine form, he revealed, would no longer be made up of the single old GE benign circle, but of three new circles, labelled Core, Hi-Tech and Services, with a bias in the latter toward financial. Membership in the triad for any GE business, as well as a continuing presence, carried stiff dues: first or second place in market standing. A rare few, such as turbines, qualified for bridging – bare-bones funding to carry the business through a temporary slump in market standing. GE businesses that loitered outside the rings, Welch said, did so at their own peril.

Foul, cried the GE traditionalists. Slough them off, and you'll make pariahs out of businesses that are basic to GE.

Anguished cries from the days of Live Better . . . Electrically. And, of course, the computer business.

But sentiment played no role in Welch's grand design. He sliced off housewares, GE's first great electrical load-building business, and the one which made General Electric a household word. He dumped big motors and big transformers, two of GE's earliest businesses. And he cast loose consumer electronics in a swap to beef up GE medical systems.

Those rebuffed businesses were core, all right, but they were skittering toward commodities. They no longer responded to hi tech, and they weren't making much money. From the very first, Welch stuck to his last: from 1981 through 1985, he divested GE of 232 businesses and product lines, while buying more than 300 others.

When GE bought RCA in 1985 for a little over $6 billion, it decided – for tax and cash flow considerations – to give RCA's David Sarnoff Research Center to SRI International, an independent research house in California. And who fielded questions for SRI at announcement time? Dennis Maxwell, their vice president for communications – an ex-A&SPer.

The "Valley Forge" years

While Welch was slimming and reshaping GE, he also de-layered. He cut out a whole management level called Sector, just one step below the Executive Office. Proud and timeless appellations such as Division gave way to amorphous names such as Business, or Operation, or Service, which now could mean that an organization was big or little, or anything. Many of the components, along with their people, slipped a notch in rank and size.

GE turbines, which was about as big and powerful as a core business could get, saw its market shrink 60% during its five "Valley Forge" years beginning in 1981. Both turbine and lamps, Welch reported at a 1986 Elfun conference, had basked in past glories and "waited too long to react to reality." They were among five of the six GE core businesses which were in trouble, he said, and if no action had been taken, "we'd be in deep yogurt now."

Staff, as one might expect, went on Welch's strictest diet, slimming down 30 per cent. Strategic planning died altogether, replaced by something called strategic management, which suggested the planning process was inherent in what operating components should be doing anyway – i.e., they didn't need extra people.

Most other staff functions – engineering, manufacturing, legal, finance, relations, etc. – stayed on the chart, but became lithe and pragmatic. The empty desks at Fairfield were enough to fire up the eyes of any real estate agent.

Initially, marketing escaped Welch's pruning at the corporate level – it hadn't appeared on the chart since 1969 when A&SP's old boss, Vice President Doug Moore, headed up Marketing and Public Affairs. After that, each GE component went its decentralized way. But when Welch set up Corporate Marketing in 1981 and brought in Vickers as vice president to head it up, he told him to create a Marketing Renaissance.

Unfortunately, Welch didn't tell him how. And that contributed to conditions which, within five years, led to A&SP's demise.

Vickers: "Join me in market making"

Vickers boldly erected a signpost for A&SP that pointed to the goal he thought was paramount: market making. "This is an exciting quest," he said. "I ask all of you to join me in the challenge."

"Great!" thought A&SPers. But some nervously noted that at the same time, Welch had sledgehammered in a bigger signpost, nowhere near parallel with Vickers', that read: money making. As Schenectady Vice President Russ Noll said later in the *GE Turbine World*: "We are not in the business of making turbines . . . we're in the business of making money."

The budding conflict, of course, stemmed from the fact that market making is long term while money making is short term. The latter, in Welch's view, was far more compelling because of his primary mission: to keep the price of GE stock high. And the gauge of that, of course, was earnings per share. The old hockey-stick promise of a return two or three years down the road was hopelessly out of date. To keep the faith with the board and Wall Street, there had to be earnings growth every year, yea every quarter.

Vickers said he welcomed Welch's goal of fundamental change. "To those who are product focused, change represents a threat. To us in marketing, it's always an opportunity." But Vickers sensed a difference with Welch in more than timing.

Six months after being named CEO in 1981, Welch had defined his preference for "marketing in its original, fundamental sense . . . making markets with relevant innovations." This seemed to hark back to his early days in plastics, which were product-focused. Then, Welch leaned heavily on R&D to come up with technological advancements which cracked open the door so that customers could be smothered with sales and application support. One couldn't quarrel much with the results; Welch had been spectacularly successful.

The problem, in Vickers' view, was that GE couldn't always rely on new products or technologies to make markets. This would often have to come from mature product lines, enhanced with the trappings of engineering and service and financial come-ons. This, according to Vickers, was the essence of market making: "Soft innovation packaging," not "manna out of R&D," nor the better mousetrap theory, trumpeted so long ago by A&SP's Stan Smith.

Welch's concepts were still coalescing when Vickers arrived in Fairfield, and hadn't yet been etched in stone. So Len proceeded to conjure up his own vision of the Renaissance.

Dave Jones: "Whither GE Marketing?"

This was heavily influenced by a remarkable 34-page document called "Whither GE Marketing?" which A&SP's Dave Jones prepared for Vickers shortly after the latter came to Fairfield. Dave was one of the few people who saw firsthand and could articulate the progression of marketing in General Electric. It stemmed from his growing-up years as one of those GE Breakfast Brats who daily soaked up the goings-on at the Works as told by an employee parent, and then, contrary to most, elected to work at the plant in spite of what he had heard. He spent all of his years with GE in Schenectady.

Dave had a distinct advantage. His father, as vice president of utility engineering, was an enlightened gentleman who helped create an enlightened climate for customers during the early days of GE. Said Dave, echoing the common sense of his father, "People are overawed by the simplicity of things." He then proceeded, first, to trace the course of marketing as it related to GE business cycles and, second, to propose what was needed, based on lessons learned.

For some 50 years up until the early '70s, said Dave, GE management was entrepreneurial, epitomizing the "risk taker and courageous business builder." Product planning, as a function of marketing, might better have been called "product happening," because output was driven more by the advancement of technology than by market demand. The marketing thrust was simplistic and effective: promote ways in which technology can improve the quality of life, then provide products that make it happen.

On occasion, when GE spotted an opportunity to either meet or create major market demands, the company did what it felt was most effective: coordinate marketing and sales at the corporate level, soliciting strong communications support from A&SP. Hence, the More Power to America and Live Better . . . Electrically programs.

Benevolent arrogance

A major competitor described this entrepreneurial role in leading the industry as "benevolent arrogance." Maybe so. But GE management felt supremely confident that GE technical leadership and product performance would convert market development investment into market share and a fair return.

Then, Dave recapped the 20-year period of decentralization, when each product department got its own marketing manager. They thought they were now liberated; in fact, they became locked into a long period of marketing decline within GE. While marketing gained peer status with engineering and manufacturing, it came in last in the competition for attention of management. This shifted from markets to the more familiar and comfortable operating functions.

There were other complicating factors. Market research, market development and advertising got short shrift. Sales and marketing often were organizationally split. Most marketing people came from the technical sales ranks, and Crotonville paid only cursory attention to marketing training beyond the pricing function. Marketing at the vice presidential level disappeared, and corporate support turned 180 degrees from outward, market-directed programs to internal efforts aimed at improving productivity – i.e., the Gopher program (Go for Improvement), etc.

In short, Dave observed, management strongly oriented itself to bottom line, fiscal year performance. In the process, the entrepreneurial spirit withered at all levels within GE. Customer wants and needs, Dave noted, "took the form of nostalgia-infected views."

Toward the end of the '60s, Dave told Vickers, GE began its third business cycle, centered on strategic planning. The fulcrum for marketing was the Strategic Business Unit, or SBU, formed of product operations with a unique mission, common market and identifiable competition. The objective was to counterbalance the focus on short-term results with that of long-range planning, and to parcel out resources to growth businesses while shutting off the flow to those at the low end.

Strategic planning shortcomings

Strategic planning never fulfilled the promise, Dave concluded, for a simple reason: "It was perceived and treated as a staff assignment independent of line operations, with principal emphasis on the upward reporting system." And, he added, the only tie between planning and marketing came from using A&SP to physically produce strategic plans and presentations. These weaknesses didn't stem from business concepts or management theory, but "from academic emphasis, biased practice, and the human tendency to forget that systems and theories are means to an end, and not ends in themselves."

And now, said Dave, GE's declared objective for the '80s is "self renewal," following a strategy of "bringing technology to market" – i.e., resurrecting the old GE "Buy and Ride" concept, where you invest in market share and then ride it up and down the life cycle. But, suggested Dave, customers may dictate otherwise. "They've suffered the consequences of over-expectation (of technology) and borne the price of failure" . . . they "demand a high degree of relevancy between the output and their wants and needs" . . . which, incidentally, "are no longer based on more, but better."

What's needed in GE marketing? First, Dave concluded, a company-wide focus on the market as the starting point of the business cycle. The environment of the '80s calls for market-driven technologies, not technology-driven markets.

Second, management must change its style from that of the internally oriented "business manager" to the externally oriented "strategic doer."

Third, strategic and tactical marketing functions should be combined at the corporate level. This allows going beyond growth or expanded scope situations to needed market development, and to highlight brand and company image.

And last, marketing skills must be uprated to offset the technical bias in GE management thinking and practice.

Vickers reviewed the concept with Welch. Back came the word from the CEO, via Vickers: "Who is this guy Dave Jones?"

Vision of the Marketing Renaissance

Dave's counsel meshed perfectly with Vickers' launching plan for the Renaissance. Vickers chose as his base point the philosophy of market-back. The needs of the market, he vowed, would determine GE's course of action. Products would be less important than the value of "soft innovations" that surround them. This put a premium on brand; push will turn to pull. Market making, said Vickers, is the true marketing function, as opposed to market sharing, which is more of a sales function. We can't just sell things, he said. To be successful, we have to solve problems in the marketplace.

For program ignition, Vickers gave A&SPers an admonition that was to become familiar: "You can't do anything differently until you see things differently." Just staring the prospect in the face, à la FOCUS, was no longer enough. "We first must gain the customer's view of the world, and then a bird's eye view of the world. Only in that way can we spot changes and capitalize on them."

Not everybody in A&SP understood at first what Vickers was saying. Often, as with Welch, it was because they didn't want to hear what he had to say. This was particularly true of Vickers' asides when he first came on scene. An early one: A&SP will be much different in 12 to 18 months. Another: All I need is a dozen good people.

His formal pronouncements were something else. I thought of Vickers during a video session at Corporate R&D with Nobel Prize winner Ivar Giaever, when I saw a photo on the latter's wall of GE's Charles Steinmetz standing with Albert Einstein.

Getting on Vickers' wavelength

The thought was triggered, through tortured logic, from a limerick I had read years before in a slim volume from Peter Pauper Press:

> There's a notable clan yclept Stein:
> There's Gertrude, there's Ep, and there's Ein.
> Gert's prose has no style,
> Ep's statues are vile,
> And nobody understands Ein.

Albert Einstein. Len Vickers. Bright as a nickel. Hard to keep up with.

Consider Len: "Marketing communications, to pinpoint the market: de facto integration of the way the company goes to market is a by-product." Or, "The market-focus idea within GE is universal and intangible . . . calls for transference and projection . . . interactive creativity with the customer." Again: "A recap of internalities that are pro market theory . . . provides another market-purposive rationale for disinvestment." Translation of the latter: We've got to be even leaner, but big and agile.

From these turgid depths, however, rose the clear-cut outlines of Vickers' Marketing Renaissance. It emerged as a two-pronged offensive: Go to Market I, a high-powered rifle to serve existing demand, and Go to Market II, a shotgun to create new demand.

The target for each: problems looking for solutions, such as industrial plant decay and rising energy costs. The genesis: customer needs, not GE wants. The plan of attack: cut through the cacophony of product department interests and highlight broad GE capabilities.

Finally, it seemed, A&SP might get the chance to help pull GE out of the communications muddle Al Ries noted some years back: "GE advertising is very good tactically. The problem is strategic."

Go to Market I and II

Go to Market I targeted high potential, emerging markets – factory automation, cogeneration, etc. GE would tailor for each a packaged offering. Where products were at parity, GE services would provide pull-through by flanking the narrow focus of competitors. This charted new ground, so ads would first search out prospects, then the GE hordes would walk them through the intricacies of the deal – typically at mini-UX conferences to be staged by A&SP.

To activate Go to Market I, Vickers thought it prudent to propose organizing the troops, not reorganizing the company – the latter would disrupt the system that shovelled up cash from the product operations. Marketing management would be centralized, for customer relations if not transactions, beginning with the bluest of the blue chips. Sales forces were to be dedicated by markets, not products. And a solution would be sought to the inevitable cross-market brokering problems – for example, GE had more organizations selling nuclear products and services than there were customers. "That's an easy fix," said Dave Jones. "Lock those involved in a room and let greed take its natural course."

Go to Market II promised several thrusts. The first would lob ads in management books – primarily *The Wall Street Journal* – to reach that elusive higher level of decision makers, to bring the word to them earlier in the selling process, and to search out influences GE hadn't yet identified. A second would realign GE Horizons at Walt Disney World as a marketing tool for the Renaissance. Another would deploy a new Business Information Center to respond realistically to cross-functional inquiries from the ads, to make it easier for people who called in to do business with GE and, of course, to gain market intelligence. In the process, the program would develop the market, build GE's brand image, and thereby enlarge its share of mind as a preferred supplier.

While Vickers excelled at conceptual thinking, he liked concepts in a form he could see, feel and touch – as one example, he visualized Corporate Marketing as an ad. So when he went to Welch in November 1982 to outline the Marketing Renaissance, he took along A&SP's highly successful cogeneration program, which had been launched two years earlier, in the Fall of 1980. It came complete with integrated promotional program, sales training, executive conference at Epcot Center, *Wall Street Journal* ad, et al. "That's the best ad I've ever seen in GE," Vickers had told Dave. "There should be one like this, with a powerful statement backed up by facts, for every area of the company."

Jousting with Welch

Vickers needed this kind of ammunition in jousting with Welch, an associate advised. With any such pitch, he warned, one of three things will happen: Welch will say "Go." Or, he'll throw you out. Or, he'll say "OK but you need more money and more people." He's never been known to do No. 1, said the associate. If the pitch is halfway good, you'll most likely end up with some form of No. 3. Which, in large measure, made up the marching orders which Vickers brought home from his visit upstairs.

A&SP held high hopes for the role Vickers saw for it as "an important part of the Renaissance." It had already slimmed to fighting trim by responding to the call of Vickers for fewer people, and from Welch for less cost. By September 1983, A&SP had dropped in less than a year from 387 people to 150. It had shut down all offices except Albany and Norwalk (later moved to Bridgeport), sent Pulver off to Florida to rev up GE Horizons, and moved up A&SP Finance Manager Frank Fagan as surrogate department manager. Frank didn't claim much advertising expertise but A&SPers instantly took to him for at least one trait – he favored "regular meetings on an unscheduled basis."

With the cogeneration program as a benchmark, Vickers unleashed Go to Market I to reconnoiter for other "big hits." Factory automation, which Welch had called an "emerging megamarket," flared briefly with an A&SP-prepared $1.6 million working trade show exhibit and 16-page insert in the trades. But it sputtered due to product and application woes, and drew back for re-arming and re-aiming. Bob Ingmire, on special assignment, explored for a year and a half the potential for an Urban Renaissance – promptly dubbed the Son of MPA – but it never found a launching pad.

At least, Go to Market I did prompt GE marketing and sales to re-orient random GE products to the single-minded pull of customer needs. Welch lauded Vickers, at an Elfun meeting, for this "strategic marketing" thrust, which activated Strategic Account Managers (SAMs) for top drawer customers, and Strategic Industry Managers (SIMs) for high gain markets, such as automotive. For those prime prospects, as well as the unwashed, Go to Market II then enhanced the image.

Launch via *The Wall Street Journal*

Corporate Marketing's Bart Snider, who was soon to join A&SP, fashioned the Go to Market II *Wall Street Journal* campaign and enlisted the Jim Johnston agency for primary support. The campaign evolved, Bart said, from an abortive automation program he and Vickers had looked into earlier for Jim Baker's Technical Systems Sector. This time, they succeeded whereas a half dozen A&SPers – such as Lou Marsh, Jack Peagler and Bob Ingmire – had tried for decades and failed to pull off an integrated corporate business campaign.

Welch was the perfect foil for the executive reader. He wouldn't put up with a long introductory rationale for the ads, à la BBDO. He assumed all the logic one might express in a preamble would shine through in the ads. If not, he'd let you know.

The initial ads, as Vickers had wanted, were problem solvers, not product pushers: "Eighty hour day" (computer-aided engineering); "Open minds, open doors" (unconventional financing); "Yesbutters don't just kill ideas" (automate to survive); etc. Later ones were fortified by a healthy dose of A&SP sourcing and first drafts: "Appreciate the depreciated" (upgrade old power plants); "A switch in time" (cut transportation costs); "In praise of mañana" (load management); etc.

The campaign of full-page ads, appearing three or four times a week in the *Journal,* worked. Eighty-five per cent of callers were first-timers; 70 per cent were not aware GE was in the subject businesses.

Not everyone cheered. A sales manager from GE's worldwide gas turbine business solemnly relayed a reader's comment about a power plant construction ad headlined "Turnkey or turkey. Only a letter apart." The plaintive comment from Ankara: "Why single out our country? It makes us look bad."

Welch vetoed a later version of the same ad, focusing on waste-to-energy plants. "Low tech," he said. Bart argued the case, but Welch won, saying, in effect: You have your constituency; I have mine.

In this, Welch acknowledged an awareness of the over-the-shoulder pull from the financial community. The ads scored in that arena. During the first three months of the campaign, GE stock jumped $9, climbing a total of $7 on days the ads ran. Volume of trading spurted as much as 16 per cent on days the ads appeared.

While the Renaissance may have flowered in Florence, it ran into some weeds beyond Padua. In producing three or four ads a week for the *Journal,* for example, Bart Snider faced a challenge that transcended the fun of television. "There are very few agency writers who really understand the businessman or the specifier . . . you can be a great writer, but you're not going to write great copy unless you can think." And an internal survey in 1986 confirmed that Bart's ads, let alone any single GE campaign, could never keep everybody happy: "The general manager wants image; marketing wants coverage; sales wants orders."

Cracking the impersonal GE shell

Customers, mostly, wanted easy access to the company. So A&SP's Bill Hewlett designed the Business Information Center to breach age-hardened walls shielding detached employees. A&SP itself had perfectly symbolized the problem in the sign-off of an ad prepared for the Service Shops. Bemoaned Roy Stratton: "It pictured the model of a generic technician, rushing to help . . . but there were no features to the face."

The Business Information Center, at least, put prospects in touch with real GE people. And this time, callers didn't get turned off by parochialism. Forty-five per cent of them, who wanted answers about a mix of unrelated products, found a GE home that had never been there before.

Other A&SPers shored up the new bridge to customers. Merle Bonthuis literally burnished the monogram, polishing so hard he squeezed General Electric down to GE, added svelte new squiggles to the logo, and upgraded company graphics in general. Dick Huether, anticipating the admonition of an IBMer that "no salesman should sell a commodity product," promoted telemarketing. *The Wall Street Journal* reported in July 1988 that GE "has more than 40 company-run telemarketing centers, plus 12 programs operated by third parties." And, in the first major apparatus handbook change in 40 years, John Wilfore shepherded a new marketing and pricing network called MAPNET. John now heads the GE Business Information Center.

Bart Snider re-examined Welch's hankering for "marketing in its original, fundamental sense." Welch had said in 1981 "I mean the attitude . . . not the function . . . the primacy of marketing as a total company perspective . . . one that shapes a company's destiny . . . everyone's issue." This, concluded Bart in a talk to the Association of National Advertisers in mid-1985, really meant that "its original, pure purpose (is) to make business more efficient. Or, in the contemporary business lexicon, to take cost out."

A hundred A&SPers agreed in July of that year when they became victims of the second great shootout. A&SP's name changed, for the last time, to Corporate Market Programs, and Dave Jones was named manager. All "make" functions, including creative, were shucked. "Buy" became the sole password.

A&SP, since Vickers' coming, had witnessed a classic turf battle, a kind of communications range war between contact and creative – the planners and the doers. When the dust settled, it was the planners who were still standing. All that remained in a sort of random corral, canted to Albany, was a cadre close to the ultimate that Vickers had envisioned. It was the end of A&SP as it had been known by the thousands of agency types who had passed through.

Down in Damage Control Central, Dave Jones assessed his chances of pulling through what was left of A&SP. He and his people no longer had to worry about chasing cat-and-dog accounts, nor even cost recovery. Its new trajectory, however, arced through the highest reaches of corporate in the sleek configuration of staff. This put A&SP at high risk.

A&SP's chances: 50-50

Dave Quincy voiced the concern of the 40 or so remaining: "We are a $3½ to 4 million cost-saving waiting for someone to discover again." Dave Jones placed the odds at 50-50.

A&SPers gave it their best. So did Vickers because, as he told Dave, he sincerely felt he could "make a difference." But more and more, the signs were wrong.

Coporate Marketing fielded a proposal to lend corporate support to GE product advertising, which was sputtering in errant independence. It would have emphasized the company's presence through horizontals and key vertical publications, and spearheaded Go to Market I thrusts. It died aborning.

The Wall Street Journal campaign, beginning in the Fall of 1984, began to span the void between customer problems and GE solutions. Gradually, the label on the lading shifted from market to product and technology. This was due to the influence on Welch of the financial community, A&SP concluded, and realistically should have been viewed as a separate issue. After a march of two years, the parade of corporate ads ground to a halt.

Hope spurted in 1985 when Welch reaffirmed that market investment was one of "the two ways to generate earnings" – the other being capital investment. As he told an Elfun gathering, "We need volume. We've come about as far as we can with cost take-outs."

Flickering hopes

The spark brightened when the Power Systems Sector agreed to be a partner with Len and Dave in a new Go to Market I venture. It was also to be a prototype for industrial and international market sorties. But corporate vetoed the funding – the sector's interests aligned more with product than with market. As usual, there was no free lunch.

The signs were not only wrong, one A&SPer observed, they smacked of the epitaph on the gravestone in an old English churchyard: "I told you I was sick."

It had become starkly clear to A&SP, and to Vickers, that there were more acceptable ways to gain volume – i.e., #1 or #2 in market share – than marketing.

Cost leadership was one way. GE had pumped nearly a half billion dollars into the 70-year-old Erie Works to beat the world, including General Motors, in locomotives and transit systems. Technological leadership was another. From an also-ran in jet engines, GE leapfrogged competition to become in five years the world's leading supplier of jet engines. And, of course, you could always buy your way to the front of the line – in satellite systems, for example, via RCA, or in diagnostic imaging systems via the swap of consumer electronics with Thomson, S.A. of France.

Obviously, Vickers wasn't the only one who needed to see, touch and feel things. Marketing didn't have the firmness of brick and mortar, the lure of the laser, or the leverage of money. Vickers and A&SP had argued that marketing, including A&SP, wasn't a cash outlay to be treated as an expense when made, but an investment like plant and equipment. Unfortunately, neither marketing nor A&SP promised the same tax advantage. And their pay-off was long-term, whereas the current corporate passion was short-term.

Last gasp: the Second Axis

In a last gasp, Vickers and Jones proposed a refinement of Go to Market I called Second Axis. The rallying cry, they said, would be anticipation rather than reaction. This would be activated by understanding – the customer first, then GE, to find out how to pull together a packaged solution to a customer's problem. This, they said, would tighten the linkage between strategic marketing and tactical selling – and in the process boost orders, optimize sales, and enhance earnings. Et cetera.

Tentatively, the proposal gained a multi-million dollar commitment, with half the amount tagged for A&SP. Two months later came a course correction: the concept was solid, but corporate still needed a multi-million dollar cut in A&SP expenses. Dave had no choice but to slash Albany and Bridgeport to skeleton staffs, preserving only 50 people in exhibits, AVCOM, and the Business Information Center.

While corporate was still de-layering throughout the company, in the Spring of 1987 it slotted in a new senior vice president of marketing and sales, a notch above Vickers. In short order, Len left the company (he's now Senior VP of worldwide marketing for Xerox), Dave Jones retired, and the remnants of A&SP, excepting those who retired or took to the outside, dispersed throughout Corporate Marketing and Sales.

AVCOM went to Marketing and Sales Support under ex-A&SPer Gerry Sheahan. The Business Information Center was welcomed in Operations by A&SP's former mentor Frank Fagan. Telemarketing found a home with Market Development and Consulting. Exhibits, along with a driblet of program managers, were assigned to Richard Costello heading a new group called – sound familiar? – Corporate Marketing Communications.

The latter, it was made clear, was not A&SP reincarnate. A&SP was dead. But the name was appropriate. Ex-A&SPers already there included Bonthuis, heading the Corporate Identification Program; Barbara Parsky, Consumer Communication; Bob Plumb, Customer Marketing Support, with Bill Hickman and Jim Harman; and, at Epcot Horizons, Pulver, Wren Aber and, later, Claudette Stroble.

Last man out

The last A&SPer to walk out of the office in Albany on October 1, 1987, was Paul Christman. Upholding the tradition of countless production directors before him, he accrued billing for five jobs still open.

In the corporate world, people are rarely fired. Said a banker in Albany, "We re-direct people." A&SP gave its people Lack Of Work notices. An LOW brought with it a three-month period of notice during which you could look for work, a week's pay for each year of service, help in printing up résumés, the advice of a headhunter, a desk and phone cozied up to other plant workers at an Outplacement Center, leads on talent scouts on the prowl from such agencies as BBDO, MCA, and so on.

For A&SPers, the Fall was illogical, unfathomable, a reversal of history. The Renaissance, instead of leading to the Reformation and an Age of Reason and Enlightenment, retrogressed to the Dark Ages.

It brought a first reaction, as with terminal illness, of denial. Two weeks after separation, I had returned to my old A&SP office for mail, when I received a call from my former boss in Bridgeport, who had also been terminated. He did not realize I had left. Even the A&SP Personnel office seemed shell-shocked – a typo in the close-out of its letter concerning LOWs chilled the hearts of the faithful: "Gook luck."

Soothsayers had long predicted the department's demise. A&SP artists Dick Savage and Bob Herr, free lancing now in Scotia, NY and Raleigh, NC respectively, recall the day they took their entrance physical in 1952 when the examiner said: "I hear they're going to break up A&SP." Production Supervisor Jim Hughes, now with Glundal Color in Syracuse, knew as early as 1982 that more than rumors were at work: "You could see it through the slowdown in people, functions and orders." A&SP management didn't need a survey to spot the drift: sheets in the GE Organization Directory binder shrank from two inches thick in 1981 to 1¼ inches in 1985.

Other A&SPers who had already left were incredulous. Said Bob Ingmire in 1985: "Can't believe all the stories about what's happening to old A&SPO/CMCO or whatever. It was fun while it lasted." Ray Bonta sent condolences in 1983: "When people ask me what I did at GE, I simply say 'I survived.' "

Schenectady area A&SP survivors gather on occasion at the Van Dyck Restaurant to reminisce. The first alumni meeting, called by Karl Ossenfort in April 1987, resembled a wake. Then, time worked its magic: the classic disaster scenario – denial followed by isolation, anger, bargaining, depression, and acceptance – ran its course, and the mood of the gathering in May 1988 and thereafter was ebullient. Most flourished in new roles, while relishing the old memories.

How fares Schenectady?

The GE Works – well, it's different. Employment plummeted from a recent high of 29,000 in 1974 to less than 12,000 in 1989. GE closed down big motors, sold insulating materials, and moved gas turbines down south. Between 1981 and 1986, the company tore down 18 buildings containing a million square feet of floor space. A year later a spokesman, ex-A&SPer Larry Stone, said GE was considering "an 84 per cent reduction" in the 195 buildings left.

One of those which disappeared without fanfare was Building 10, housing the workshop in which Edison started the Schenectady Works. All is not lost, however. For $20, the Elfun Society will sell you an actual brick from the workshop, complete with a brass plate etched with a sketch of the building.

Schenectady? Just fine, thank you

How fares the town itself? Fine, thank you. The Schenectady Economic Development Corporation recalls that in 1974 the county population was 64,000 with five per cent unemployment. In 1988, the figures changed to 72,000 and 3.1 per cent. The latter is the lowest in a decade, and the current problem is a shortage of skilled labor.

The plant is no longer the bustling, self-contained community it was in A&SP's glory days. Efficiency now is the watchword. The employee stores and the library have been closed, the interplant bus line stopped, and services such as mail, medical, police and fire protection have been contracted out, via sourcing. Personal bonds dwindle. Shortly after leaving, I called the GE insurance office about picking up a benefits brochure at the plant. "You can't," the voice responded. "We're in a secure area. I'll mail you one."

Shades of Kurt Vonnegut. "Player Piano II"?

Schenectady management, at least, recognized it had a morale problem. So to mount an employee motivation program, one component called on – two ex-A&SPers who had just been released on LOW. Their theme for the program: "The GE family . . . changing for the better." The client, who himself earned an

LOW shortly thereafter, scratched his head and said: "I don't like the last part. It's too upbeat."

Impact on served clients

And what of the company? Did the demise of A&SP have any lasting impact?

Clients bemoaned the loss of specialized services – for example, distribution, including mailing list maintenance, etc. But these were quickly picked up by other GE service components, or outside vendors. More than that, clients missed the program management skills of A&SP, the planning and integration of copy and art and production. One who yearned for A&SP most, strangely enough, was a service division finance manager. "We can't get any more cost out," he said. "We have to get more business, which means spending not at the top line but the bottom line."

It was hard to measure the impact of A&SP's departure on advertising volume. An analysis showed that of the $396 million GE spent in 1984, only 24 per cent – discounting sales promotion, co-op, publicity, exhibits, etc. – was for true advertising. Corporate and consumer made up three fourths of that, leaving $24.5 million to prop up $21.5 billion in sales – a penny in advertising for every $100 in sales. This was A&SP territory, but on its departure the flow of ads was so low and so diffuse that one could scarcely notice the difference.

The "wet finger" method showed the decline that had already occurred. Bound volumes of A&SP ads measured three inches thick in the 1946 edition, then swelled to two volumes of five inches in 1956. Others skipped around a range of from three and four inches until 1969, when they began a decline to less than an inch in 1977. There, the records stopped.

The listing of ad insertions for 1986 which GE provided to its agencies – this time including RCA ads – doesn't look anemic. A shade less than 6,000 pages of ads appeared in 812 publications, ranging from *Mortgage Banking* to *Mother Jones,* from the *International Bottled Water Association* to *Incider* (hic!), and from the *Harvard Business Review* to *Heavy Metal Hot Shot.* Playing no favorites, GE placed 10 pages each in *Playboy* and *Playgirl.*

Major casualty: knowledge

The biggest hole in the GE fabric was rent by A&SP knowledge slipping away. Said one corporate project manager: "Our major challenge is to find people who understand and are sensitive to GE goals and practices." A product department ad manager, about to begin a new business-to-business campaign, echoed the lament: "I asked for credentials from this major agency. They sent me a Michael Jackson poster and commercials for Pepsi and Geraldine Ferraro."

Some kicked off the learning process anyway, counting time and frustration as the trade-off for a fresh viewpoint. Others simply kept working with A&SPers as they struck out on their own, or moved to set up their own firms on the outside: Light & Power Productions. Center Stage. Masto-Dagostine. Keats, design. CRD Graphics. Createacor. Tradefair Productions International. AWT Business-to-Business Communications. Banks Marketing Communications. ICOM. The list goes on.

This placed them firmly in the groove of comfort and capability that A&SP outsiders, both client and agency, had enjoyed for years: Armtek's Bob Jones, for example, inviting Lou Marsh to help with corporate communications in New Haven; Coleco ad manager Harvey Johnson looking to Doug McKinlay for agency services through McKinlay & Partners in Simsbury, CT. Et cetera.

A nagging question remains: Would A&SP have fared any differently under another regime?

It's not likely. A&SP has always tracked the course of GE and GE has gone, as Reg Jones noted, "where society takes us." Today, it's taken the company into a very different world – an understatement in the mold of Carl Ally. If GE had stayed where it was in the '70s, it would likely not even be around today. At the least, it would be slogging along in the sorry image of other big companies which waited too long to change, such as U.S. Steel and U.S. Rubber.

As GE changed, so A&SP did, too. It changed when Ralph Cordiner inherited from Charlie Wilson a company the former said was dedicated to "security, complacency, and mediocrity." A&SP changed when Fred Borch and Reg Jones introduced strategic planning; then, the department vowed loyalty to marketing, ignoring the fact that there was a deep chasm between planning, which became essentially a staff function, and operational marketing. And, of course, A&SP transmogrified with Welch.

Can management get away with such drastic changes? Why not? The corporation is citadel to the last of the monarchies. The king, the CEO, can do just about anything he wants, as long as he swears fealty to the inviolable – stock price and earnings per share. On GE's current course, it could wind up as a bank, or even a merchandiser, the ultimate result from the ploy of sourcing.

The answer to the first question begs a second: Will A&SP recoup and reappear?

Probably, in some form. One can still spot functional A&SP pockets within GE. But it's unlikely they will ever regroup and charge forward as the massed A&SP formations did 10 or 20 years ago. It would be wholly out of context – in Durant's terms, "forever clinging to the old beliefs . . . tinkering with obsolete armor."

A new A&SP would probably spring from a seedbed of computers and telecommunications, much as that in the GE Business Information Center. It would be nurtured this time by electronics rather than print, forming an intelligence center to monitor the interchange between product departments, sales forces and customers. It would be the ideal place for a small number of A&SP planners to spot trends, and to suggest changes in market strategy via the "bird's-eye view" Vickers envisioned.

Advice for the next A&SP

The new A&SP, however, would do well to mix in a few doers, well versed in the company, along with the planners. A&SP's original mission was communications; this could apply to marketing, but also to sales, or to public affairs, or any GE function. That's the context in which A&SP earned its reputation, excelling at a select few skills which were not readily available on the outside. Bob Fegley listed them for his old alma mater at an A&SP Regeneration Forum in 1973:

First, to crystallize options and force decisions. It's amazing, said Bob, how many GE managers "have no idea what they stand for, what they want to do, and what message they want to get across to their audience, including their own associates in the business." Get it down in black and white. The result – whether an ad or a speech or an article – may seem "more like a negotiated treaty than a work of art" but it will represent a "new order of understanding" compared with the battlefield from which it came.

Second, to blend contradictory objectives and interests into a coherent position or message. GE is like nature, said Bob – a "soft slurry of paradoxes," with many diverse though interrelated parts, plus built-in contradictions. It is up to A&SP – sometimes hammering it out with a sympathetic lawyer – to present a plausibly unified message.

Third, to help move the company toward its larger goals. Avoid the hired-gun complex, warned Bob, that makes one pursue narrowly conceived objectives. Move in from the periphery and help customers see the bigger picture that is GE.

Last, to lift language and art to the level of power. That, said Bob, is "the fundamental expectation." But don't "equate creativity with cleverness . . . (or) get carried away with the gimmick and lose sight of the business objective." The best A&SP communications, he said, achieve their goal with "clean and graceful efficiency."

Of course, there may never be another A&SP. But there will always be the affectionate thoughts of those who were with it during the years when it played a central role in the selling of General Electric.

Late in 1986, a year before A&SP's long decline came to an end, a group of GE marketing and sales people meeting in Fairfield exulted at the remarkable company wares and capabilities that were now available to the business community. A GE senior vice president, who left the following year to join another firm, wistfully wondered: "Why haven't we told this story?"

CREDITS

Advertising Age, August 1982, 158.
ADWEEK, March 1984, xi.
Ibid, 113.

Bernbach, Bill, reference re: Robert Rees, Doyle Dane Bernbach, at GE A&SP March 1, 1978, 90.
Brower, Charles, *Advertising Age,* July 30, 1984, 58.
Burnham, David Hudson, *Bartlett's Familiar Quotations,* Little, Brown & Company, 1980, 24.
Business Week, March 16, 1981, 124.

Calkins, Earnest Elmo, *"and hearing not . . .",* Charles Scribner's Sons, 1946, 80.
Caples, John, *Tested Advertising Methods,* Harper & Brothers, 1932, 146.
Century of Progress, Hall of History Foundation, with the Elfun Society, 1981, 45.

Durant, Will, *The Story of Civilization,* Simon & Schuster, 147, 186.
Dun's Review, October 1968, 3.

Electronics, February 19, 1987, 169.
Elfun Society mailing, November 18, 1986, 183.

Faulkner, William, from the *Paris Review,* in *Bartlett's Familiar Quotations,* Little, Brown & Company, 1980, 41.
FOCUS, General Electric Company, 1976, 147.
Forbes, May 28, 1979, 112.
Fortune, February 11, 1980, 84.

Gibbon, Edward, *The Decline and Fall of the Roman Empire,* Limited Edition Club, The George Macy Companies, 1946, 20.
Guidelines for Creativity, General Electric Company, 1976, 147.

Hopkins, Claude C., *My Life in Advertising,* Harper & Brothers, 1927, 38, 142.
Hurwitz, Henry, Jr., *Schenectady Gazette,* February 9, 1987, 68.

Industrial Marketing, October 1979, 7.

Kroll, Alex, per GE's R.O. Stratton, 1979, 147.

Langley, Edward, the *New York Daily News,* as quoted in *The Wall Street Journal,* May 4, 1981, 60.
Limerick Book, The Peter Pauper Press, 174.
Linn's Stamp News, December 17, 1984, 145.

Madison Avenue, September 12, 1988, 156.
Mad magazine, E. C. Publications, Inc., 59, 87.
McCall, David, Association of National Advertisers, 1977, 147.
McGraw-Hill Magazines, 73.
Media Report, released to GE/RCA advertising agencies, March 24, 1987, 184.

Newman, Edwin, at GE Creative Services meeting 1978, 154.
New York Times, The, October 8, 1972, 5.
Ibid, May 5, 1985, 78, 167.
Ibid, May 3, 1987, 111.
Ibid, November 16, 1986, 156.
Noll, Russell, *GE Turbine World,* February 1987, 170.

Ogilvy, David, *Confessions of an Advertising Man,* Macmillan Publishing Company, 1963, 146.
Osborn, Alex, *Your Creative Power,* Charles Scribner's Sons, 1950, 119.

Parkinson, C. Northcote, *Parkinson's Law,* Houghton Mifflin Co., 1957, 165.

Reeves, Rosser, *Reality in Advertising,* Alfred A. Knopf, 1976, 146.
Reflections, 50th Anniversary, the Elfun Society, 1978, Schenectady, NY, 46, 80, 139.
Ripley, Charles M., *Life in a Large Manufacturing Plant,* 1919, published by the GE Publication Bureau, 46.

Schenectady Economic Development Corporation, July 8, 1988, 183.
Schenectady Gazette, December 22, 1986, 168.
Ibid, January 23, 1986, 183.
Ibid, March 11, 1987, 183.
Snider, Hubert M., *GE Advertising: 30 Minutes Worth of the First 75 Years,* September 15, 1977, 4, 31, 37, 79.
Snider, Hubert M., *Marketing & Media Decisions,* 1985, 162, 178.
Snider, Hubert M., Association of National Advertisers, September 9, 1985, 179.
Stein, Gertrude, per Robert M. Pirsig, in *Zen and the Art of Motorcycle Maintenance,* Bantam Books, 1988, 147.

Terence, *Bartlett's Familiar Quotations,* Little, Brown & Co., 1980, 148.
Thurber, James, *The Years with Ross,* Atlantic-Little Brown, 1959, xv.

Vonnegut, Kurt, Jr., *Player Piano,* Dell Publishing Company, 1952, 125.

Wall Street Journal, The, March 30, 1987, 56.
Ibid, December 7, 1988, 56.
Ibid, July 5, 1985, 78.
Ibid, July 6, 1987, 118.
Ibid, September 25, 1985, 168.
Ibid, June 6, 1988, 168.
Ibid, July 21, 1988, 178.
White, E.B., *The Elements of Style,* with William Strunk, Jr., The Macmillan Company, 1959, xv, 18, 146.
Whitney, Dr. Willis R., 1930, in *GE-100 Speakers Resource Packet,* 1978, 46.

Zwart, Elizabeth Clarkson, *Des Moines Tribune,* 127.

INDEX